THE UNOFFICIAL X-FILES COMPANION II

THE UNOFFICIAL X-FILES COMPANION II

N. E. GENGE

AVON BOOKS ◆ NEW YORK

Photographs on pages 49, 104, 124, 130, 145, 180, 193 copyright © Fox Broadcasting Company/courtesy Everett Collection
Photographs on pages 1, 39, 59, 69, 75, 81, 91, 171, 202, 209 copyright © Fox Broadcasting Company/courtesy Photofest
Photographs on pages 6, 136, 171 copyright © Globe Photos, Inc.
Photograph on page 112 copyright © National Geographic Society/courtesy Everett Collection
Photograph on page 177 copyright © 1980 Columbia Pictures Industries, Inc./courtesy Everett Collection
Photograph on page 150 copyright © Warner Bros./courtesy Everett Collection

THE UNOFFICIAL X-FILES COMPANION II is an original publication of Avon Books. This work has never before appeared in book form.

AVON BOOKS
A division of
The Hearst Corporation
1350 Avenue of the Americas
New York, New York 10019

Copyright © 1996 by N. E. Genge
Interior design by Stanley S. Drate/Folio Graphics Co. Inc.
Published by arrangement with the author
Library of Congress Catalog Card Number: 96-31486
ISBN: 0-380-79024-6

Library of Congress Cataloging in Publication Data:

Genge, Ngaire.
   The unofficial X-files companion II / by N.E. Genge.
      p. cm.
   1. X-files (Television program)   I. Title.
PN1992.77.X22G47   1996   96-31486
791.45'72—dc20   CIP

First Avon Books Trade Printing: December 1996

AVON TRADEMARK REG. U.S. PAT. OFF. AND IN OTHER COUNTRIES, MARCA REGISTRADA, HECHO EN U.S.A.

Printed in the U.S.A.

QPM   10 9 8 7 6 5 4 3 2 1

For Peter,
  who, every day, makes me a little
  more grateful for having met him.

Acknowledgments

Once again, I'm delighted to acknowledge the able assistance and generous contributions of the many people who've helped bring this collection together. I might have been able to do it without you—but it was a lot more fun with you.

For directions to all things curious or peculiar, and the more remote corners of the stacks, the staff of the Queen Elizabeth II Library of Memorial University (St. John's), the medical library at the Health Science Center (St. John's), and the Raymond J. Condon Memorial Library and Resource Center (Labrador City), with special thanks to Alexandra Hartman, Sandra McDonald, Beth Woodman, and Patricia Ho.

For sharing bandwidth and insights, the Covert Group—you know who you are.

For their continued assistance in separating fiction and reality, the patient people who form the Public Relations staff at the Federal Bureau of Investigation. Ray, for the tour off the beaten track—especially the basement! Paul, for sharing my curiosity and a lifetime's worth of experiences in the field. Elaine, for "girl talk" about everything from arrogant bosses to the proper shoes for a prolonged foot chase.

For laughter, guidance, and the best calamari, two wonderful people who just happen to be terrific agents, Ling Lucas and Edward Vesneske, Jr.

For generously providing her expertise on short notice, Debbie Nathan, author of *Satan's Silence: Ritual Abuse and the Making of a Modern American Witch Hunt*.

For making a long-distance project as comfortable as if we'd shared the same hallway, my editor, Stephen S. Power, and his colleagues at Avon Books, especially Michael Murphy, for being there when it counted.

And, for everything else that made this book possible, including wry wit, a willing ear, broad shoulders, and the ability to create calm amid the chaos, my own rock, Peter.

Contents

X – REFERENCE

X-Cultures   25

X – REFERENCE

Yet Another Alphabet Organization?   95

Introduction

Without change, performers, writers, directors, even audiences get bored. For the staff of a product like *The X-Files*, which strives to present more than the latest special effects, which consistently attempts to create original television and recast even established story lines in a new light, which takes the relationship between its leads into more demanding areas than the bedroom, change comes in somewhere above oxygen on the list of necessary things.

Unfortunately, just as change provides unexpected opportunities to stretch the parameters, as *The X-Files* did so successfully during Anderson's second-season pregnancy, it can also provide a bumpy ride for viewers—especially a viewership who has proven as loyal to a concept as X-Philes have undoubtedly been. Not surprisingly then, season three, which presented changes both subtle and dramatic, created something of a love-hate relationship with viewers.

Some of the changes, and their influences, were obvious. Talents like Darin Morgan, Kim Newton, and John Shioban, whose distinctive touch on a script makes credits almost redundant, delighted with their humor, their compassionate portrayals, and their eerie characterizations of even the most depraved "bad guys." Yet, while their contributions added another layer to a program already "dense" with self-reference and allusion, not everyone was dissatisfied with the *old* formula.

Viewers who'd hung off their chairs, terrified, during episodes like "Ice" and "Tooms," and who'd tuned in for more of the same, could easily find episodes like "Syzygy" and "Clyde Bruckman's Final Repose" a bit outside their established tastes. Humor?

Likewise, viewers who preferred conspiracies and UFOs, plotlines adhering tightly to the internal mythology developing within *The X-Files'* universe, might describe excursions into the mysteries of religious faith, as in "Revelations" and even "Teso dos Bichos," as nothing more than "filler to show between the good stuff."

Walking fine lines, however, is an established X-Filean maneuver.

In its three years on air, *The X-Files* has struck an ofttimes uneasy balance between originality and tradition. Imitation is still the sincerest form of flattery, and, in season three alone, *The X-Files* has "flattered" everyone from Stephen King ("Pusher") to Fyodor Dostoyevsky ("Talitha Cumi"). While the sources of their inspiration are evident—and usually acknowledged on screen—some twist, some unique combination of cameras and action marks the new product as distinctly *X-Files*.

By combining such apparently diverse topics as alien abduction, monsters of the week, and even "ordinary" humanity exhibiting its most bizarre side, *The X-Files* pulled in devotees of what are actually incredibly diverse areas of interest. On another program such "inclusiveness" might have resulted in a product that failed to really satisfy anyone. On *The X-Files* characterization is as strongly focused as plot and, by combining the best of straight drama with the traditional strengths of the science fiction and horror genres, a remarkably talented cast and crew carry viewers across wildly divergent circumstances with an internal consistency that ties the whole together.

Without that internal consistency, season three, which jerked audiences from "The Walk's" sheer terror to the fractured hilarity of "Jose Chung's *From Outer Space*," could easily have sent confused viewers channel-surfing.

Instead, departures from the established formula energized *The X-Files*. Viewership swelled. The media ate up anything and everything connected with the show. Merchandizing went wild. The term "X File" joined the ranks of popular parlance and, somewhere between "Anasazi" and "Talitha Cumi," the cult hit became a mainstream smash.

Was that designation nothing more than a media designation? Or will it tangibly affect what we see on screen? "Style" and "tone" aren't easy to quantify. Separating the influence of individuals from an overall trend is even more difficult and, after all, some deviation from the original premise was inevitable.

If Mulder remained as puppy-dog cute, as naive, as incredulous as he appeared in the pilot episode, or if Scully wandered from autopsy to autopsy, from one incredible event to the next with no perceivable reaction, audiences would rightfully scream, "Foul!" Well, they would if they hadn't already lost interest and switched channels.

However, after making the allegiances of characters like Skinner, Krycek, and various members of the Mulder and Scully families murky enough to leave viewers scrambling for their scorecards, the X-crew could hardly be blamed for exploiting the loopholes they'd left so conveniently open. If that exploitation took the plot in unexpected directions, then they'd simply done their job well.

Oddly enough, the unease about the program's incredible popularity is often expressed not in terms of grand conspiracies, but in the details.

"How many times can they work 'son-of-a-bitch' into a third season script?"

Obviously, more often than they did in the entire first season.

"When did Scully become such a prude?!"

Somewhere between discovering Mulder's attraction for a woman named "Bambi" and finding him under the maybe-not-so-natural-blond Detective White? Or was it just before she declared an extra-marital affair sufficient cause to suspect Skinner's mental state had become unbalanced? Certainly not when, during the first season, it was revealed that, even as a student at the Academy, she'd been sufficiently confident to conduct an open affair with an instructor.

"Since when did they have to spell it out for us?"

Since, sometime between "Anasazi," when the collective minds behind *The X-Files* decided that a few blurry frames of film would alert their attentive viewers to the tunnel between Mulder's burning boxcar and freedom, and the end of "Talitha Cumi," when they literally unscrambled P-A-L-M on screen.

No one is denying that significant changes occurred just as the program hit "the big time." The writing team of Morgan and Wong, responsible for such fan favorites as "Die Hand Die Verletzt" and "Ice" left to pursue their own projects. Chris Carter himself was busy pitching and preparing his new series, *Millennium*, during much of *The X-Files'* third season. New faces joined the ranks. Others, like David Duchovny, hankered for a change of pace.

Whether the show's progression was a deliberate attempt to appeal to a wider audience composed less of astute viewers attracted to a challenging hour of television than of excess-cash-spending demographics, or simply the natural evolution of a product that is, after all, an expression of a very human cast and crew, is probably a moot question. What the third season, with its experimental and original stories and presentation, has undoubtedly done is expand the X-Filean borders as the series moves into its fourth season.

Where will that fourth season take us? If *The X-Files* continues to explore the limits of what can be presented in an episodic format, in terms of stories, dramatic presentation, cinematography, and, yes, even special effects, the result will be television that not only tickles the minds of its ardent fans, but seriously shakes up the notion that "genre" programming can't compete head-to-head with mainstream dramas.

That more changes are in the offing is a given.

No longer will the eerie chords of *The X-Files*' theme echo through living rooms on Friday nights. That time slot, which played such a major role in the program's development, has been taken over by *Millennium* which, if Carter holds true to form, will demand a considerable percentage of its creator's time, time previously lavished on *The X-Files* exclusively.

Duchovny, anxious to keep the film career that looked so promising prior to taking on an episodic role going, has reportedly asked for a lighter time commitment in season four.

Mitch Pileggi, who gained lead billing this season—only to disappear for months at a stretch—has been signed to a long-term agreement.

Darin Morgan, story editor for much of season three, was talking "burn-out" and a "change of scene" as "Talitha Cumi" was tucked into the can.

With *Space: Above and Beyond* an unfortunate casualty of the ratings game, Morgan and Wong have returned to *The X-Files*' stable; however, their attention will also be divided between *The X-Files* and *Millennium*.

Once again, new ideas, circumstances, and personalities will find expression, and, if season three is any guide, X-Philes had better sit back and be prepared to expect the unexpected!

THE UNOFFICIAL X-FILES COMPANION II

Code Name: "ANASAZI"

CASE SUMMARY:

A decades-old conspiracy pulls Mulder and Scully into its complex snare when a mysterious fourth Lone Gunman surfaces with information capable of proving the government's intimate knowledge of alien visitation. The problem? No one can read the files! Masked by the only unbreakable code known to modern history, the files lead Mulder and Scully to a Navajo reservation and a forgotten boxcar.

EYEWITNESS STATEMENT:

"I think it's just encrypted, and I think I recognize it. It looks like Navajo. It was used during World War II. My father told me that it was the only code the Japanese couldn't break. I—I remember the long strings of consonants."

—Special Agent Dana Scully

Guess this piece of evidence was a bit too big for a specimen bottle in the Pentagon basement.

Code Talkers: Finally Speaking Loudly

Eighty-five-year-old Navajo men, tested in the hellish theater of World War II's South Pacific, are still known to awaken confused, drenched in cold sweat, and terrified by dreams of Anglo teachers and the dark, coarse lye soap that could nearly choke any child who dared speak the soft language of the Dině, the Navajo People. If viewers found a certain irony in Skinner, Assistant Director of the FBI, entrusting the Scullys to Albert Hosteen—the government asking the Indians for protection—they can certainly appreciate the real-life irony of asking the Navajo to use their language to protect soldiers of a government who'd spent years denying its value—or the value of its speakers.

However, the same Navajo who'd spent generations adapting to new technology while fending off attacks from both local tribes and Europeans couldn't refuse the opportunity to defend the land between the Four Sacred Mountains—even if that land was currently within the United States.

The first group of recruits faced stiff challenges. Like all other Marines, the future Code Talkers were dragged from the comforting familiarity of home, dumped into a boot-camp system that emphasized a conformity all too reminiscent of the hated white schools, and put through tough physical and mental conditioning. Not surprisingly, the physical qualifications posed little difficulty. Adjusting to the "routines" and overcoming cultural differences took more effort, but were hardly outside the abilities of the first all-Navajo platoon. They graduated together, after setting range records, and moved on to their "real" assignment without any idea of *why* they had been recruited in the first place.

Once past the shocking revelation that the Marine Corps *wanted* them to create a code based on the Navajo language, the first recruits settled down to business with a vengeance. First an alphabet, then a code within a code began to emerge, no small feat considering the significant fact that Navajo had no natural words for normal military parlance. Tanks, colonels, M-1's, and switchboards were as "alien" to them as any extraterrestrial could be. While few non-Navajo had even

TRIVIA, BUSTER 1

X-Philes had four months to contemplate the events of "Anasazi," so don't expect any of these questions to qualify for *easy* trivia points. Every one of these is a two-pointer. Good luck!

1. In what Navajo community did the Hosteens live?
2. What piece of sports gear was shaken off Eric Hosteen's dresser when the earthquake hit?
3. What did Eric Hosteen's grandfather, Albert, suggest he leave alone the morning after the earthquake?
4. How strong was the "trembler" that rocked the Hosteen residence?
5. What was The Thinker reading when he broke into the Department of Defense computer?
6. Quick! How many languages other than English were spoken during this episode?
7. Who did The Lone Gunmen believe was following them?
8. How did Frohike describe the shooting in Mulder's building?
9. Which Commandment did Mulder direct Scully's attention to?
10. What does The Cigarette-Smoking Man consider to be an inevitable consequence of life?
11. What words did Scully's source manage to decode for her before she turned the documents over to Albert?
12. What did Scully steal from Mulder after he fell asleep in her bed?
13. How high did Mulder's temperature go during his night at Scully's?
14. What did Scully find in Mulder's water tank?
15. Where did Mulder find himself after Scully took him on his cross-country, waterless ride?
16. Where did Mulder claim to have spent the last few days while "chatting" with The Cigarette-Smoking Man?
17. A plate on the side of the boxcar revealed the name of the company that originally owned it. Which line was it?
18. What did Mulder find on the arms of the "aliens"?
19. Name the agent who began the testing on Mulder's gun.
20. What was one of the chemicals Scully suggested might explain Mulder's bizarre behavior?

a pidgin knowledge of the language, communications based solely on an existing language couldn't satisfy the need for secure contact over open radio frequencies. Instead, by assigning Navajo words to *represent* other Navajo words, then using that reworked lexicon as the basis for communications, the Code Talkers could completely bewilder even other Navajo.

Naturally, the Code Talkers found it necessary to prove they could deliver what they claimed, a cipher system capable of communicating information swiftly and perfectly. The typical Marine Corps system involved a complex machine which would encode the message based on that particular day's parameters, transmit the resulting encoded communiqué to the recipient, who would then have to decode it in like fashion. Because these messages followed no real language rules, errors in transmission became evident only when, hours later, the decoded message made no sense. In test after test, the Code Talkers produced perfect "translations" of the original messages—instantaneously. The implications for a nation facing Japan's talented cryptographers as well as her soldiers were enormous.

Even with their primary objective, a highly functional encryption system, achieved, the Navajo continued to face difficulties in the field.

ANSWERS:

Remember, *all* these answers are worth two points.

1. Two Grey Hills, New Mexico.
2. A basketball.
3. Snakes.
4. 5.6.
5. *50 Greatest Conspiracies of all Time*.
6. Four: German, Japanese, Italian, and Navajo.
7. A multinational Black Ops Unit, code-named Garnet.
8. Weirdness.
9. Number 4.
10. Regret.
11. "Goods"; "Merchandise"; "Vaccination."
12. His gun.
13. 102.
14. A dialysis filter.
15. Farmington, New Mexico.
16. The Betty Ford Center.
17. The Sierra Pacific Railroad.
18. A smallpox vaccination mark.
19. Agent Kautz.
20. LSD, amphetamines, or an exotic form of dopamine.

YOUR SCORE _____

Like their colleagues in the ranks, they endured the misery of battles throughout the Pacific: Guadalcanal, the month-long and foot-by-foot fight for all five miles of Iwo Jima, the dreaded beach assault at Okinawa and every craggy little island in between.

The Code Talkers also discovered their own, unique problems. More than once, they drew "friendly" fire. Apparently, distinguishing a Navajo man from a Japanese man was beyond the discretion of some Marines. For the majority of Marines, who didn't understand a single word of the hundreds of thousands transmitted by their Talkers, Navajo sounded suspiciously like Japanese—especially in the dark. It wasn't any easier for the Navajo men captured by the enemy! One man spent months of his confinement convincing the Japanese he was Navajo-American, not Japanese-American. Discovering that it was the Navajo who were responsible for the "gibberish" stumping their intelligence efforts didn't help. He spent the remainder of his confinement tortured for answers he simply didn't have. The "Navajo" he was hearing was as much gibberish to him as to the Japanese—exactly as intended.

The exigencies of war required the Code Talker language, like any other natural language, to expand as new weapons, tactics, and geography were encountered. As group after group passed through the Code Talker school, the dictionary grew. Original members often did their "homework" in foxholes instead of in classrooms. Keeping abreast of new terms could mean life or death for thousands of men, and the Code Talkers seldom had the luxury of leaving their units. In the four years of the Code Talker program, the original 263-word dictionary nearly doubled in size to over 500 terms. Unlike other codes, the Navajo Code was never written down anywhere outside the training school. There was no cheat sheet taped to the sides of their radios and telephones. Taking advantage of the Navajo's verbal tradition made that possible, and added an extra layer of security to the system, but certainly it made the Code Talker's job in the field tougher.

Not unique to the Code Talker program, but the bane of all communication and encryption efforts, were "leaks." Secrecy, which had been impressed on the Navajo themselves from the beginning of the project, was being breached back home. Several papers, as well as monthly magazines, ran stories on the Navajo contribution to the war effort.

While most were satisfyingly vague, at least one went into consider-able detail. Though breaking the code still seemed impossible for all practical purposes, *any* information provided to the enemy endan-gered not only the Code Talkers, but the men whose messages they were passing.

That need for secrecy didn't end with the end of the war either. The Cold War erupted almost before Germany surrendered, and the United States was wondering if she wouldn't be hip-deep in another war, this time with the Soviets, before she could settle the situation in the Pacific. While the armed services were unlikely to abandon a sys-tem that worked as well as the Code Talkers, the possibility of another, immediate conflict made the Code Talkers even more valuable assets. Unlike their comrades, who could release some of the horror of the conflict through formal and informal discussions after the war, the Navajo were still sworn to secrecy years later. For them, there could be no carefree bar chat, no pillow talk, no explanation of what they had done to help end the war. Responsible for the most sensitive messages, the Navajo Code Talkers were frequently present at the most important strategic meetings and the first to know where and why major offen-sives would occur; yet, because of the nature of their work, their contri-bution to history and their unusual perspective on those momentous decisions were lost for nearly thirty years.

While Carter racked up an acting credit, Duchovny was adding story credits to his resume.

eXtras:

É Í 'AANÍ Í GÓ Ó 'A HOOT'É: THE TRUTH IS OUT THERE.

X

The theory behind double encryption is deceptively simple: Take an original message, encode it, then pass that message to a second person for a second encryption. Of course, any regularly repeating set of characters can be decrypted by reversing the process—which is both the challenge and the weakness of ciphers.

If you've ever attempted to learn a foreign language, however, you already know that real languages, as opposed to codes, have irregularities that speakers recognize, but that often ignore the "rules" or grammar of the language. Then, in addition to intentional abuses of the language's system, there are the absolutely incomprehensible "idioms." Things like *mon petit chou chou*, an endearment to the French, but "my little cabbage" to the rest of us.

Languages, subject to the whims of speakers separated by geography and experience, are by nature more complex than any code. Combining as complex and relatively unknown a language as Navajo with the encryption expertise of the National Security Agency resulted in one of the few unbroken "codes" in security history. Though *The X-Files* focused on the involvement of the Navajo during World War II, in the previous World War some dozen Native American groups took part in the Code Talker projects.

During World War II, the Navajo Code Talkers performed perfectly, with not a single missed or incorrectly interpreted message.

X

Want a peek at Chris Carter, the creator of *The X-Files*? He's the agent at the end of the table during Scully's interrogation scene.

X

Hosteen, as in Albert Hosteen, the fictional Code Talker in "Anasazi," isn't the most common name. It was, however, shared by one man who was well aware of the Code Talker program. Dennie Hosteen, a New Mexican Navajo, was among those who helped rip Iwo Jima from Japanese control. He, too, was a Code Talker.

Code Name: "THE BLESSING WAY"

CASE SUMMARY:

Dana Scully's partner is missing, probably dead. Her career, three years of struggle and sacrifice, is ending in failure and humiliation. With her resources limited to the paranoid Lone Gunmen, a distant band of Navajo chanters, and her own initiative, she couldn't have picked a less auspicious time to encounter an enemy with a full-generation head start.

EYEWITNESS STATEMENT:

"Beware these men, for they are dangerous themselves—and unwise. Their false history is written in the blood of those who might remember and of those who seek the truth."

—Albert Hosteen, Navajo Elder and Code Talker

DEEP BACKGROUND:

Majestic-12

In an example of art imitating life imitating . . . well, at least one man's vision of reality, *The X-Files* "borrowed" one of the Holy Grails of UFOlogy, updated it for the 1990s, and began a tension-filled game of hot potato. Rumors of a single, massive set of files detailing military and political involvement in a UFO cover-up stretching from Roswell to the Persian Gulf War surface from time to time, titillating the imaginations of those who dream of a decisive answer to the UFO question. Bluebook, the Yellow Pages, MJ, Majestic-12 . . . The code words and their objects vary, but the basic story remains, and if it reflects earlier tales, so much the better for a television program about alien abductions and government intrigues.

The current incarnation, the Majestic-12 version, hints at a set of filing cabinets, not quite as extensive as the "lots and lots" of files in *The X-Files'* mountain hideout, but totaling either a dozen, sixteen, or twenty-four four-drawer units—depending on which set of "authentic" documents you read. If even one document proves legitimate, however, then the entire history of alien contact is locked inside some big metal drawers eight floors under the main offices of the Central Intelligence Agency. The contents of which would fit rather neatly on one generously sized DAT tape!

If we believe everything reputedly found in those files, proof of alien cultures became available to the American government in early 1939, when pilots were followed for six hours by obviously alien "hovering craft" that made "no attempt to disguise themselves" or "avoid detection." Alien remains surfaced in 1943, when one of those "hovering craft" failed to hover and was observed falling into the ocean. The

TRIVIA BUSTER 2

Easy Stuff: *Give yourself one point for each correct answer.*

1. Where do The Cigarette-Smoking Man and his associates hang out when they're in New York City?
2. Name one of the two dead men who "spoke" to Mulder as he lay unconscious in the Navajo hogan.
3. What was in the canister dropped into the boxcar while it was full of "aliens"?
4. What did a doctor remove from the nape of Scully's neck?
5. Where is the Mulder family home located?

Tougher Trivia: *These are well worth their two-point value.*

6. What is Dana Scully carrying in her hand when she arrives at her mother's house?
7. Who did Frohike call a "redwood among mere sprouts"?
8. Frohike brings Scully a newspaper article about the death of Kenneth Soona. From what paper did it come?
9. What was Melissa's friend, Dr. Pomerantz's, specialty?
10. Where was Bill Mulder buried?

craft survived and was recovered—with a complete, but dead, crew. A reasonably intact spacecraft was shipped to the Nevada proving grounds from Roswell in 1947. And a living, breathing alien (with an inexplicable taste for strawberry ice cream) traveled to a dozen different sites before it died a natural death on June 2, 1953.

So how was all this accomplished without the knowledge of the American people?

As every good conspirator knows, from inside a "shadow government" whose contacts put both Deep Throat and X to shame.

These documents, though frequently "protecting" key witnesses by providing false names, or providing them anonymously, nevertheless don't pull any punches. Starting at the very top, they identify the President, whoever the current occupant of that title might be, as "Majesty," and "Operation Majority" as the overall code name for any and all activities relating to alien contact. Majority siphoned off physical evidence, hushed witnesses, and ensured that even within its elite circle of supporters, information seeped back out only on a need-to-know basis.

An elaborate system of projects and personnel supported Majority's many ongoing activities. The "Grudge Collection" handled the paperwork. Everything that ended up in those filing cabinets passed through Grudge's scrutiny. Some documents simply disappeared into crisp manila folders. Others found their way into more active sections.

ANSWERS:

1. Forty-sixth Street. Take two points if you get Forty-sixth and Tenth Avenue.
2. Deep Throat and William Mulder.
3. Oxygen cyanide.
4. A tiny computer chip.
5. West Tisbury on Martha's Vineyard, MA.
6. Her shoes.
7. Mulder.
8. *The Examiner*.
9. Psychotherapy, hypnotic regression, and energy fields.
10. The Garden of Reflection in the Parkway Cemetery of Boston, MA.

YOUR SCORE _____

Keep track of your progress and find out what kind of agent *you* would make.

Even half-dead, Mulder still wants his version of "comfort" food

Take the Garnet Berets, the team tracking Mulder through the "Puerto Rican jungle," rally-driving down mountainsides, and generally preventing him from hanging on to his evidence. They'd have felt quite at home in Project Garnet, the arm of Majority responsible for ensuring the security of project papers and personnel—at any cost. There was no shortage of either.

Communicating with an alien culture, especially with topics as sensitive as abduction, technology exchanges, and hybridization on the agenda, challenged even the best diplomats. "Sigma" provided specialists to establish original communication protocols, continuing as spin doctors capable of producing convincing press releases on demand, along with terrific forgeries of official documents to support any government position. Once the language barrier was broken, the basics of an agreement established, "Plato" reintroduced the envoys in hopes of improving the government side of the deal.

Eventually, according to Majestic documents and proponents, the Platonian Corps secured a treaty agreeable to the handful of power brokers allowed knowledge of the negotiations. The terms were reasonably simple. In exchange for alien technology and absolute secrecy about its origins, Majority, through its agents, Majestic-12, allowed periodic "harvesting" of humans and domestic animals. The aliens, however, didn't get full access to the population. Majority demanded a "periodic accounting" of the "subjects." The aliens readily agreed to provide reports—after the fact.

Project Aquarius tackled the human end of the deal, the flood of technology supposedly filling American labs and intelligence operations, including a detailed history of alien involvement with this planet, all carefully squirreled away under what some UFOlogists believe remains the ultimate in security classifications, MAJIC. Among its many subprograms was "Pounce," designed to recover future crash debris—including any alien passengers—while "Pluto" recovered the less tangible evidence like eyewitnesses and whatever scraps of proof they'd communicated to anyone else.

Aquarius's main thrust, of course, remains the conversion of alien theory and crash rubble into an *operating* craft. That's where "Redlight" and "Snowbird," the overall disinformation wing of the operation, become part of the Majority web. If Area 51 watchers, the FOIA gofers, and modern Deep Throats are credible witnesses, Redlight succeeded in getting its first joint human-alien craft off the ground in 1952. It promptly blew up. The project quieted down again as everyone went back to the drawing board, but rumors of the event began spilling out to the watching UFO community and Snowbird went into high gear. Snowbird's only real purpose, to provide as much disinformation and as many alternate explanations as possible, resulted in a half-dozen different, but conventional, aircraft attempting test flights in and around the very areas UFO watchers designated as the most sensitive. Considering the instability of *any* conventional aircraft without wings, there's no obvious reason to even bother with these prototypes, a fact that only reinforces the belief among some watchers that their real purpose is to confuse the evidence trail they think leads to proof of alien contact.

However, not everything went smoothly in this extraterrestrial alliance. It seemed the aliens had forgotten to mention a few pertinent points, among them the fact that, while strawberry ice cream was nice, they needed specific human body parts to supplement their diets. With more abductions making the news, more reliable witnesses doing the reporting, and careful UFO investigators making connections to a bizarre series of cattle mutilations, hiding the alien presence was getting tougher. In addition, the aliens were getting sloppy themselves, returning individuals whose memories hadn't been properly wiped. Like Duane Barry, they might remember the tiny implants secreted beneath their skin, or, like Dana Scully, they might discover them accidentally and link them to their memory lapses.

Suspecting their control was slipping, or that it had never been as firm as they believed, the government side scheduled one of only three general meetings ever to gather Majestic operatives in a single room. The guest list, if real, was impressive. At the top of that register, MJ-1, always the current Director of the CIA, answerable only to the President. MJ-2 to MJ-12, select heads of government and civilian bodies including the National Security Agency, the State Department, the Defense Department, the Joint Chiefs of Staff, and the Federal Bureau of Investigation itself. Among those who've supposedly served as MJ-2 to MJ-12 are Nelson Rockefeller and J. Edgar Hoover, who met with their compatriots in—where else?—midtown New York City. You just can't get much more midtown than the Forty-sixth Street chosen by *The X-Files*.

According to Majestic lore, the only man ever to have turned down a position in the organization was none other than John F. Kennedy. (Well, it had to tie in, right?) It was supposedly just weeks after voicing the unpopular opinion that all this should be laid before the American public that Kennedy died in Dallas. Maybe in the X-Filean universe, The Cigarette-Smoking Man really did "see Presidents die."

For the remaining members of the Majestic group, however, it was business as usual: commandeer, contain, and control. Except this time it was the aliens that needed containment. Heading a list of antialien weapons *Star Trek* would kill for are "Joshua," "Gabriel," and "Excalibur." Low-frequency pulsed sound guns, missiles capable of penetrating the hundreds of meters of rock required to reach the aliens' "hidden bases," and "beam" weapons for any lingering underwater alien presences. Even the Strategic Defense Initiative, more popularly known as Star Wars, has been implicated in the Majestic plot as Project Zeus, a name not completely unfamiliar to X-Philes as well as conspiracy proponents.

While many elements of the "Majestic" scheme recur in any number of UFO-related theories, Majestic is perhaps the most all-encompassing, far-reaching, and international of the lot. There is no social ill, from drugs (supposedly the source of funds for the UFO experiments) to AIDS (a human-alien medical procedure gone wrong), it can't encompass. With Majestic linked to legitimate aerospace projects, and the United States engaging in numerous joint projects, almost any country could be a coconspirator. And, in a subtle chicken-and-egg scenario, any attempt to discredit Majestic is easily ascribed to Snowbird and, in a roundabout way, actually supports the existence of this "Above Top Secret" project!

If that scenario couldn't be parlayed into material for a program dependent on its viewers' healthy curiosity and modern distrust of government, the crew behind *The X-Files* would be less than the storytellers they've proved themselves to be.

eXtras:

Scully's neck implant seems increasingly plausible in light of the "tracking bracelets" used on convicts and the "identification disks," actually microchip dots, that are rapidly replacing canine tattooing and dog tags.

X

Larry Wells, to whom this episode is dedicated, was *The X-Files'* costume designer.

X

Trap and Trace Trust *The X-Files* to ignore Ma Bell's phone-tracing ability when convenient, yet have a major plot point tied to her ability to do the previously impossible! The handy c-phone, completely untraceable when Scully was abducted, led The Cigarette-Smoking Man's henchmen straight to her on a deserted highway. In order for Ma Bell to "find" a cellular phone when there's a call, it must trace its whereabouts; and, of course, it does just that whenever a cellular phone is turned on. By tracing the "cells" the signal passes through, Ma Bell can fairly easily judge the general area of any c-phone, regardless of whether anyone is using it.

Blooper Alert! Mulder's exit wound healed before the entry wound—despite the fact that an exit wound is normally four or more times larger than the entry.

 Blooper Alert! Was it Mulder, Scully, or Skinner who took a break from an intense, three-way Mexican standoff to close the blinds in Mulder's apartment?

Code Name: "Paper Clip"

CASE SUMMARY:

Together once more, Scully and Mulder follow a fifty-year-old trail to a Nazi-turned-gardener brought into the country under the shelter of Operation Paper Clip. His claims, including a theory Scully swears isn't remotely possible, nearly divide the partners yet again before leading them to truths much closer to home.

EYEWITNESS STATEMENT:

"We are operating sooo far outside of the law right now . . . we've . . . given up on the very notion of justice. We've turned ourselves into outsiders, we have lost our access and our protection—"

—Dana Scully

DEEP BACKGROUND:

Under American Noses: Operation Paper Clip

Operation Paper Clip wasn't nearly as covert as *The X-Files* implied, but its supporters certainly wished it had been, and with good reason. Just at a time when the American public was horrified by tales of German atrocities, American strategists found themselves almost desperate for an opportunity to pick the brains of Germany's top scientists.

Germany's surrender suddenly left America and her allies with widely divergent problems instead of an adversary dangerous enough to force cooperation. Individual nationalistic interests came to the fore almost before the bombs had stopped falling. Their "enemy at home" defeated, Soviet, British, and French leaders were desperate to "normalize" life for a population all too used to sacrifice. The Americans, however, had come to the particular attention of the Japanese. European thoughts turned to rebuilding; American psyches, still stunned by Pearl Harbor, still facing a serious Pacific threat, scrambled in an effort to maintain their supremacy.

The Soviets, victors amid rubble, began stripping Germany's infrastructure almost before the Germans knew they'd lost. Streetlights, auto factories, even breweries were dismantled, packed aboard hastily repaired rail lines, and shipped home.

Britain, too, had "boys" to employ at home, citizens clamoring for lost luxuries, and industrialists anxious to use German innovations in facilities returning to peacetime ventures. They had few objections to employing the German minds, mostly industrialists', that had made Germany a major contender in world markets. United Kingdom citizens had watched refugees flee Hitler even before the invasion of Po-

TRIVIA BUSTER 3

Easy Stuff: *Give yourself one point for each correct answer.*

1. Who did Mulder ask to watch over Melissa Scully?
2. Who eventually ended up with the DAT tape containing the MJ files?
3. Whose mathematical constant was the "key" to the vault in the mountain?
4. Name the American policy that brought Nazi war criminals from Germany to the United States just after World War II.
5. What is Samantha Mulder's middle name?

Tougher Trivia: *Two points each for these challenging teasers.*

6. Victor Klemper's favorite flower?
7. Which man hugged Mulder in this episode?
8. What does Mulder threaten to leave Frohike in his will?
9. What company used its premises to create the country's largest underground filing cabinet?
10. Where did Mulder and Scully find "home-cooked meals" after escaping from the mines?

land. Accepting that just being German wasn't evidence of harboring Nazi sympathies, Britain welcomed the scientists, who promised a swift return to prewar comfort and prosperity.

Even France managed to carve out an enclave ripe for exploitation when her weary citizens were ready to reclaim and reconstruct their society.

Americans had their own problems.

Yes, Germany was defeated, but what of her ally Japan?

Just as German scientists had joined Americans to work on the Manhattan Project and at Los Alamos, creating what the American military was already calling the "ultimate weapon," their colleagues back home were persistently rumored to be close not only to their own atomic device, but also to dozens of other advanced weapons. Considering the destruction caused by the V-1 and V-2 rockets, the havoc wreaked by Germany's "big guns" like Bertha, and the mobile devastation that rolled across Europe with the panzer divisions, these "rumors" kept the night-lights burning and antacids flowing in a significant portion of Washington, D.C.

The necessity of discovering the extent of German potential, what they'd shared with Japan, and how soon the United States could expect to confront these "superweapons" in the field was imperative.

But how?

German directives ordered the destruction of documents, models, and facilities that had to be abandoned. The advancing Allied troops had neither the training nor the time to protect sensitive documents.

ANSWERS:

1. Albert Hosteen.
2. Former agent Alex Krycek.
3. Napier's.
4. Operation Paper Clip.
5. Anne.

6. Hybridized orchids.
7. Frohike.
8. His video collection.
9. Strughold Mining Company.
10. Charlotte's Diner.

YOUR SCORE _____

In an explosion of joy and hatred, liberated civilians often obliterated any reminder of their oppressors.

Reconstructing what was left, even in the rare instances of completely untouched sites, could take years—years the States didn't have.

Finding the native German scientists wasn't difficult. Hundreds actively sought out Americans, offering their knowledge for nothing more than the safety of their families and a few thousand calories of food a day! Others were rounded up without resistance at their places of work. Even more arrived in response to requests from co-workers already in the American Zone. A few guerrilla-style forays into the zones occupied by their allies—before the official establishment of an international board, of course—was sufficient to locate the remaining German minds.

Attempts to utilize this rich resource of "intellectual reparations" in Germany itself were impractical. After all, their labs, notes, and material were already being shipped back across the Atlantic! There were few facilities for families in the camps. Many wives and children lived in bombed-out homes that were looted repeatedly. In the basically lawless days after the surrender, roaming gangs murdered hundreds of suspected Nazi sympathizers on less evidence than the Nazis themselves had used to round up dissenters. Muddling the scene further, the scientists were actively recruited by other Allied governments. Hanging on to its specialists couldn't be easy for Germany when the Soviets and British were offering lucrative work contracts, superior facilities, and—most importantly—citizenship!

It was the citizenship issue that Paper Clip was designed to circumvent—and which caused knee-jerk reactions back home in the States. Having been flooded by the horrific images of skeletal figures limping out of the camps, John and Jane Q. Public took "Not in My Backyard" to the extreme. The very notion that America needed mutilators of human flesh—or their compatriots—was instinctively abhorrent.

Constant reassurances that these men weren't war criminals did little to sway anyone's opinion—with good reason.

As Americans feared, the screening process admitted some rather "questionable" immigrants.

Among the most famous is Klaus Barbie, former Gestapo officer.

While many scientists could honestly claim that membership in the Nazi party was a meaningless requirement, Barbie wasn't one of them. Barbie's Gestapo rank was by no means honorary. As chief of the Gestapo at Lyons, he personally sent thousands of French and German Jews to the concentration camps. He was responsible for the murder, and torture, of resistance fighters and formal prisoners of war. As an intelligence officer for a pro-Nazi political party, he aided his colleagues' covert travel both back to Germany as France fell to the Allies and from Germany to Africa and South America when Germany itself teetered on the brink of defeat. Although his American recruiters carefully documented his background, affiliations, and activities, they offered him a job instead of a trial.

Another recruitee was responsible for an atrocity that went beyond the almost mundane matter of murder, deliberately striking at the Jewish soul. In a twisted take on Judaic law, Otto von Bolschwing, former SS man and later CIA operative, swept through Bucharest, driving its Jewish citizens ahead of him into a meat-packing plant where they were hung from meat hooks and branded as "Kosher Meat." Considering the quantities of blood at the site, ankle-deep in places, it's likely most of the victims were alive as they were flayed. One, a child of no more than five, had her throat slit, a desecration of the kosher laws von Bolschwing was playacting out. In 1945, when German defeat was evident, von Bolschwing offered himself to the Americans as an intelligence expert, a position he retained for decades.

Literally dozens of programs, some more successful than others, contrived to bring Germany's scientists and intelligence officers to America, or at least to deny them to the Americans' former allies. Operation Pajamas brought a distinct set of specialists, those Germans involved in the forecasting of European political trends, to the United States. Project Birchwood concentrated on "economic experts," men who'd worked under Goering in conjunction with the SS. Project Dwindle imported Nazi cryptography equipment and the men who created the algorithms. Apple Pie, a project cosponsored by the British, plucked Germany's "Soviet specialists" from the ranks, and a solo American effort, ironically called Project Credulity, continued the effort. The smuggling of bioengineers, doctors, veterinarians, even dentists and pediatricians into the country under these and other programs would inevitably lead to the question of why these men hadn't been admitted under the normal immigration regulations.

Considering that history proves the rocket scientists, the missile experts, and the intelligence operatives were all utilized to the maximum, the premise behind "Paper Clip"—that no matter what the biological and chemical scientists did, it would also be seamlessly integrated into America's labs—isn't that difficult to believe.

eXtras:

Strughold Mining Company The name Strughold has its very own file in the real Operation Paper Clip. Not a place but a person, Professor Hubertus Strughold was one of the first to enter the U.S. under the protection of Operation Paper Clip in 1947 with the enthusiastic support and the full knowledge of Colonel Harry Armstrong, a wartime surgeon of the U.S. Eighth Air Force.

Himself a specialist in aerospace medicine, Strughold had worked in the Luftwaffe's Aeromedical Institute and in the Physiological Institute of the University of Göttingen before leading a group of fellow scientists to the American Zone.

Among the scientists whom Strughold brought with him were Dr. Hans Clamann (a specialist in the construction of low-pressure chambers and high-pressure cabins), Dr. Ulrich Luft (leading researcher in the adaptation of diet, nutrition, and breathing to high altitudes), Dr.

Ernst Opitz (coronary physiologist), and Dr. Otto Gauer (specialist in the physical effects of acceleration on the human body).

While these scientific immigrants were carefully screened before their arrival, many Americans were decidedly uncomfortable with the possibility that human experimentation on unwilling POW, Jewish, and other concentration camp victims was part of their research.

Those doubts were quickly proved valid when thousands of German documents were unearthed, many of which later appeared at the Nuremberg trials. Though Strughold's scientists claimed to have carried out their experiments on mice, dogs, and pigs—and the American researchers studying their facilities did indeed find equipment of a suitable size for rodents or small cats and dogs—no chambers, no pressure gear, no ice tubs, in fact absolutely nothing large enough to hold a pig was ever found. The rest of the experimental setup had been found months earlier, at Dachau, where *human beings* were subjected to pressure enough to pop eyeballs, temperatures that killed in less than thirty minutes, and ice baths colder than anything the pilots whom this work was supposed to have aided would ever face. The "pigs" referred to in all the reports were, in fact, Jews who refused to abandon keeping kosher.

Strughold, however, was never tried in connection with any of his European work. Nor were any of his nearly thirty colleagues. After moving to Texas, the group formed the core of the Air Force's first Department of Space Medicine, a "shining example of American ingenuity" and an "example of where future aerospace studies could take us."

Mario Mark Kennedy, to whom this episode was dedicated, was an active on-line fan, running a chat forum on America On-Line, and well known for his discriminating commentary. He died in 1995 from complications arising from an accident earlier in the year.

X

 Blooper Alert! If Mulder and Scully were depending on Napier's constant to get them into that vault, they were out of luck. Napier's constant is 2.71828—not the 2.7828 Scully and Mulder used to open the lock.

X

 Blooper Alert! Mulder's memory, reputed to be near photographic, appears to have failed him in this episode. Although the mountain vault files clearly read "Samantha Anne," which the X-File Mulder himself opened, and which Scully read way back in "Conduit," gives his sister's middle initial as "T."

X-REFERENCE:

X-Cultures

When production companies delve into cultures not their own, they take a risk. To get it "right," they risk losing an audience that's either uninterested in or oblivious to the layers of meaning being added to the final product. If they get it wrong, someone will undoubtedly pick it apart—tossing out an entire story line for the sake of a few details. And if the unthinkable happens and more than a few details get flubbed, they risk offending an entire ethnic group just at a time when Hollywood is being held to higher standards than the producers of spaghetti Westerns ever had to worry about.

Of course, it's difficult to offend people who, like the Anasazi, haven't walked the earth for nearly a thousand years. When no one knows much about them, it's almost impossible to "get it wrong." Give a bunch of curious X-Philes a real-life ancient mystery and *five months* of nothing but reruns to distract them, however, and you can almost guarantee they'll begin digging, trying to find its deeper meaning in the X-Filean universe, and return well informed by the time Part II airs.

The first item a curious X-Phile discovers is that, strictly speaking, the Anasazi aren't Anasazi. Taken from the Navajo for "Ancient Ones" (as defined in the X-Files universe), the people we call Anasazi undoubtedly had a different, if lost, name for themselves.

Even the cliff dwellings so long associated with them probably don't present an accurate record of their lifestyle. Before drought drove them back to the cliffs, the Anasazi built their towering communities, their huge hogans, and their amazing waterways in the open, where they could see for miles in any direction. Pueblo Bonito, one such open-plain community in the Chaco Canyon area, remains as an example of their close-quartered cities. And cities they were. Among Pueblo Bonito's three acres stand four- and five-story, free-standing buildings on well-planned streets. Seven thousand Anasazi lived here, peacefully from what evidence remains, content to share walls and floors with their neighbors.

Seven hundred years before Christ, Anasazi achievements reached a startling level of accomplishment. The bow and arrow replaced inefficient spears, cotton was grown and woven into exacting patterns, architectural techniques included interlocking masonry, craft arts like pottery embraced dozens of differing techniques, and decorative arts enjoyed a similar growth. Refinements continued for nearly two thousand years with carefully managed agricultural resources supporting a steadily growing population. The early notion that the Anasazi may have "eaten themselves out of house and home" in retrospect appears unlikely. From burial remains and the relative size of family dwellings, the Anasazi may, in fact, have practiced a very effective form of birth control. Few families exceeded four children, and child mortality seems to have been low. Considering their harsh environs, the Anasazi may have been incredibly talented agronomists, very much in tune with what their ecology was capable of supporting.

By 1300, however, the massive, efficient cities were empty.

When the cities were first surveyed back in the 1800s, their resemblance to the cliff dwellings was less understood, and for some time even professional archaeologists believed the Anasazi had simply disappeared.

Later, with the history of the Southwest considered as a whole, Anasazi influences were found in dozens of other sites, including Ácoma, Laguna, Hopi, and Zuñi. Climatological history indicates that between 1250 and 1300, drought may have been a serious motivator to abandon the open plains. If estimates are anywhere close to accurate, in that fifty-year period less than a half foot of rain fell over Anasazi lands. For a people dependent on agriculture, it meant devastation. That they survived at all remains almost as mysterious as their eventual disappearance.

Given the profusion of conflicting histories and theories, the X-Crew can probably be forgiven for the odd academic slip.

One thing, however, is clear. Art and pottery weren't the only things they shared with their neighbors. The great kivas of the Anasazi, the hogans of the Navajo, and the religious ceremonies of these and other tribes prove there was, at some time, a widely practiced religion with many more points of similarity than difference covering a large part of the Southwest. In that sense at least, the Navajo traditions explored in the three-part arc of "Anasazi," "The Blessing Way," and "Paper Clip" are indeed a reflection of those "ancient ones."

But how closely did *The X-Files* mirror modern, more easily researched Native American tradition and ceremony? Though the details of rituals and lifestyle occasionally veered from the accepted, the atmosphere produced by the crew and cast echoes a time and place most North Americans will never have the opportunity to witness.

The Legend of the White Buffalo

I was privileged to have the able assistance of Charles Little Deer of the Lakota Nation in assembling this particular rendition from the collected verbal tradition of several Native American archives, including the Navajo, Lakota and Rosebud Sioux, and the Cheyenne. Any errors are strictly my own and unintentional.

"White Buffalo Woman" transcends cultural boundaries among many Native American communities. While the story differs in detail, it remains an enduring source of hope, a hope that found its way into non-Native cultures with the birth of a white buffalo calf named, aptly enough, Miracle. To understand the powerful pull the rangy little calf exerts over so many, and to appreciate just how closely *The X-Files* adhered to the tale, requires some understanding of the legend behind the symbolism.

> Sun pounded the heads of the Sioux People and the game ran from its fierce presence. For the People, it was a time of great suffering as empty bellies cried out for food. Even the plants shriveled and died. Women and men cried over their hungry children.
>
> Gathering their best weapons and water, two men set out to travel farther than they ever had before. Sun followed them and they grew sick and dizzy. Three more days they walked before finding a small spring. They drank deeply and slept. The younger man dreamed of a beautiful woman who sang to him. Her song thundered with the sound of a thousand buffalo hooves.
>
> Morning came and the men awoke to the sound of a woman's voice singing. The men looked up and saw a woman walking toward them from the east, out of the rising sun. She was beautiful. The younger man recognized her from his dream and warned the older one that this woman was strange and wonderful. The older man looked upon her with desire.
>
> As the woman came nearer, the younger man saw that she floated above the ground. He heard the sound of the buffalo in her song. Dressed in white buffalo skins, she outshone the sun with her beauty.

The older man did not heed the young man's warning and tried to touch the strange woman. The wind rose. A cloud formed over the man. It fell to the earth and hid him from sight. When the wind had blown it away, all that remained was a pile of bones.

The young man covered his face, but the woman sang again until he was no longer afraid. To him, she said, "Go and tell the People that I will come to them soon." It had taken five days to reach the spring and he had seen no food, but the man agreed to go back. On the first day, he caught a fat rabbit. On the second day, he found a partridge dragging a broken wing. On the morning of the third day, he found his village.

At first the People were afraid of the woman's coming. The young man told them of her beauty and her powerful song. He showed them the bones of the rabbit and the partridge. The People were no longer afraid.

The next morning a woman walked out of the east. She wore white buffalo skins and carried a bundle in her arms. The People welcomed her and shared what little food they had. To the People, she said, "I have come to teach you a new way, a way that will take away your hunger and make you strong."

The woman unwrapped the bundle. Inside was a sacred pipe which she gave to the men. After teaching them prayers to rise with the smoke, she said, "With the pipe, you will become a living prayer." The men learned the words and smoked the pipe.

Then the woman gathered the women around the fire. To them, she said, "You are of Mother Earth. Your way is hers. What you do is important."

As the sun set, the woman allowed the men back into the circle around the fire. She reminded them all of the power of the pipe. She taught the men to value the buffalo, to value their women and children. Then she sang for them. The sound of buffalo hooves was loud in her voice. She sang of the hunt. She sang of the bravery of the buffalo. The women sang with her, and their song was loud and carried over the land.

She stood and began to walk away. At the edge of the village, she stopped. "I will return again to renew my faith with you. Remember me." Her feet rose with each step until she floated high above the horizon. The People watched as she turned herself into a white buffalo calf and disappeared with Sun.

The Sioux remembered the words of the White Buffalo Woman. They honored their pipe and the buffalo came. They used the buffalo wisely and could feed the women and the children. The women remembered the songs and taught them to the children, who taught them to their own children. As they met others of the People, they heard the songs of the White Buffalo Woman sung around their fires and knew there must be peace between them.

Over the years, the Legend of the White Buffalo has taken on an additional layer of meaning for many Native Americans, as well as for non-Natives who've begun exploring the history of their adopted home. In addition to laying down a set of environmental and family living standards any modern people could take pride in, the Legend is also credited with preserving peace between otherwise warring groups on the Plains.

When Miracle was born on August 20, 1994, many Native Americans regarded it as symbolic, a sign that their culture—their unique ways and rich history—might finally enjoy a rebirth even within the larger non-Native society. For as monumental a task as uniting all of humanity in peaceable accord, the tiny, scruffy, demanding little calf was a rather ludicrous ambassador, at least at first glance.

Sharing their farm in Wisconsin with a living legend certainly wasn't on the To-Do list of the Heider family. In fact, the constant stream of visitors, both Native and non-Native, could easily have started a whole new source of friction. As news of the event spread, the Heiders were inundated with sightseers and serious pilgrims alike. For people who'd never heard of the White Buffalo Woman legend, the attention was, to say the least, disconcerting. For the Heiders, like most non-Natives, Miracle's birth was their first introduction to Native culture.

As thousands came to see the one-in-six-million miracle-calf, however, media outlets broadcast the legend not only across the United

States, but into almost every country with a Reuters newsfeed! To date, Miracle's visitors hail from locations as diverse as Australia, Mozambique, and Ireland. If Miracle's purpose in life was to bring humanity together and promote the history of the Great Plains tribes, she's earning her keep! And unlike the unfortunate calf in *The X-Files'* version of the tale, Miracle's mom is still happily chewing her cud. If Miracle lives as long as the last recorded incarnation of White Buffalo Woman, the clumsy calf still has about thirty-six years to get her message, her truth, out there.

The Blessingway

With their religious significance, the Blessingway scenes carried an even higher emotional load, and a heavier responsibility to "do it right."

Under television's tight constraints, it'd be nearly impossible to represent the detail and intricacies of such a complex ceremony on-screen, but within those limitations, *The X-Files* created images surprisingly evocative of the original. And considering that, even among the many Navajo Chant Ways, the Blessingway chant remains different in form and intent, that was no mean feat.

If compared to modern medical practices, the Blessingway chant falls loosely into the realm of preventive care. Most Navajo Chant Ways address existing problems, but the Blessingway is a spiritual vaccine against ill health, chance bad luck, unpleasantries, and even poor emotional health. From a culture that emphasizes the importance of family, community, and an individual's balance, it might even be thought of as a communal blessing, a way to reinforce those ties in a positive way.

Though all the elements were present, from the four-poled hogan to the drypaintings, fasting, and song, the Blessingway chant itself seemed oddly out of place for Mulder's needs. The Blessingway rituals, really the basis of all the other ceremonies except Enemyway and Monsterway, are certainly reflected in the Healingway chants, but the Blessingway itself has nothing to do with healing an existing illness. Blessingway ceremonies would be more appropriate for a woman expecting a child, teens heading out of the community for extended periods of time such as a university term, or newlyweds.

The treatment of the dead is a delicate subject in most cultures, and the Navajo Nation is no exception. In fact, if there was one area where *The X-Files* seemed to have chosen a story line completely contrary to that of the Navajo they were hoping to reflect, it was in the treatment of the dead and dying.

The Navajo abhor the early end of a life, considering it more than unlucky. Bringing Mulder, apparently dying, into a family's hogan constituted a serious risk. If, as they seemed to expect, he'd actually died, they'd have no choice but to abandon the hogan forever. With some functioning hogans estimated to have been in continuous use for centuries, and still considered the center of even modern homes, it appears unlikely the family would subject Mulder to a ceremony not designed to improve his health in a place not meant to house the dying.

Likewise, the initial incident bringing the boxcar of "aliens" to Mulder's notice smacks of the subtly wrong. It seems highly unlikely that a young Navajo man would bring a dead body to the home of his obviously traditional grandfather. Or handle it himself, for that matter.

However, these inconsistencies—among the rich history the program managed to get very "right," the additional layers of meaning that many X-Philes had spent the summer coming to appreciate, and the unique setting the program was able to re-create in as unlikely a place as southern British Columbia—certainly aren't enough of a flub to invalidate a damn good story.

NOTE: In a piece of serendipity, yet another Vincent Scully, not the voice of the Dodgers, whom Dana Scully was named for, but an historical architect, is currently working on the Chaco Canyon and other Anasazi sites.

Code Name: "D.P.O."

CASE SUMMARY:

When a small town chalks up its fifth lightning-related death, Mulder suspects something is amiss in rural America. Despite her own inability to find any errors in the autopsy proceedings or results, Scully can't help but agree with her partner's assessment when a suspect jump-starts his boss's heart—bare-handed.

EYEWITNESS STATEMENT:

"Did you know that lightning kills several people a year at home, in the shower or on the phone? That people have seen it dancing on the ground like balls? That scientists will tell you, if push comes to shove, that they really don't know what makes lightning work at all?"

—Sheriff Teller

DEEP BACKGROUND:

When Sparks Fly . . .

Sheriff Teller joined an exclusive club in "D.P.O.," as one of the few ever to catch Scully with her intellect down. That crack about her "homework" must have stung—especially when the topic was lightning and Scully's undergrad degree *was* supposedly in physics. Perhaps the character should take solace from lightning's bizarre place in history, fiction—and the lab.

Whether it's the spark jolting Frankenstein's monster to life or Thor's thunderbolts, imagination seems the only limit to the fantastical abilities people attribute to lightning. As if a force capable of discharging 10^9 joules of energy while turning sand to glass weren't supernatural enough . . .

Maybe if science could actually explain all the peculiar phenomena associated with this eccentric and dynamic form of electricity, the writer's curiosity would be satisfied. But how do you explain away centuries of scientifically sound observations that add up to absolutely zip?

Take ball lightning, for example. It defies all the conventional wisdom. It never streaks from convenient point to convenient point. Instead, it might roll languidly down the aisle of an airplane, as it did on August 12, 1956, where it was observed by two experienced pilots, three law enforcement personnel, and a meteorologist heading into the airport as holiday relief for the facility's own weatherman. Shaken, they reported "a brilliant ball of light, slightly less wide than the space between seats," that "hissed like snakes" as it bounded down the narrow area and disappeared without a trace through the rear fuselage.

Occasionally, the odd trajectories ball lightning can move in con-

TRIVIA BUSTER 4

Easy Stuff: *Take a point for each correct answer.*

1. What video game started the fight between Jack Hammond and Darren Oswald?
2. Darren's buddy went by an unusual first name. What?
3. What was Connerville's bizarre export product?
4. What unusual item did Scully and Mulder find in the melted sand?
5. Sharon Kiveat flunked Darren in what subject area?

Tougher Trivia: *Two points for each of these.*

6. For what company did pizza delivery boy, and victim, Jack Hammond work?
7. What was Darren Oswald's middle name? (Half points for getting just the initial.)
8. What did Darren Oswald offer Sharon Kiveat as a snack?
9. What did Mulder find in Darren's magazine, between Miss April and the Women of the Ivy League?
10. Name one of the three models of car Darren offered to steal for Sharon Kiveat.

vincingly mimic intelligence. Mrs. Petra Daley, of Dunnellon, Florida, enjoyed spending the typical midday downpours on her front stoop until a ball of lightning appeared out of nowhere, followed her twice the length of the porch, and popped right through her screen door as she fled inside. It left a perfectly circular hole in the mesh before chasing her upstairs to the bathroom, where it finally disappeared by "exploding with a bang like someone shot off a rifle." Like 10 percent of those who've had close encounters with ball lightning, Mrs. Daley reported nausea, memory loss, and disorientation. Perfectly normal reactions to a severe electrical shock—except there's no physical evidence that she, or any of the others, was involved in a lightning strike!

Even so-called "ordinary" lightning keeps scientists hopping. "Bead," "chain," or "pearl" lightning, a brilliant lightning stroke that collapses into segments and was once believed to be an optical illusion, was finally caught on high-speed film in 1992. Finally, there have been reports like those of the English crew of the *Mary Joe*, who claimed to see "tracer fire" over the bay of their peaceful village during a thunderstorm. The "official" report had concluded the men had been watching too much coverage of the Gulf War on telly—despite the fact that two of the crewmen didn't even own a TV.

Of course, even casual observers' reports gain some credence when enough independent accounts describe similar events. Colored lightning, in hues covering most of the spectrum, came to the attention of stupefied scientists only about once a decade, but the anecdotes echoed one another faithfully. The August 1890 event in England mirrored another from Nevada in 1993 right down to time of day, 07:15, weather conditions, clear skies, and colors, "for the most part, reddish to orange, but one flash, the largest observed, appeared as one streak inside another, yellow with a blue streak through the center." Recent theories suggest that red, the most common color reported, results from hydrogen being released from water vapor along the length of the streak, but the rarer colors, greens and combinations, remain a mystery.

If color, a supposedly simple and observable phenomenon, still stumps science, imagine the twists that lightning's truly bizarre performances put into a carefully established theory.

Lightning is supposed to strike things like tall trees, office buildings, and conveniently placed lightning rods, right? Certainly that's the usual pattern. Nearly three dozen Hereford citizens would dispute that, though. While attending a boot sale, they observed a streak of lightning descend from overhead clouds, turn sharply, then bypass a clock tower, two church steeples, and hosts of chimneys to strike the home, some four miles distant, of a Mr. Isbell, who lived in one of the lowest points of town. Bet he was wondering whom he'd upset!

Mrs. Lillian Hermes, longtime resident of Vancouver (home of *The X-Files*), was carrying a stack of dishes in from the car when lightning slammed into an oak on the lawn behind her. In addition to the damage inflicted on the tree, every plate was smashed, yet not a hair on Mrs. Hermes's head was disturbed, despite the fact that she was between the tree and the dishes.

When people and lightning actually come in contact, things get even weirder. On a stormy night in 1904, in a churning North Atlantic, lightning slammed into the ocean and into the *Galicia*, en route from Hamburg to St. Thomas. Leaning forward to peer out a side window, the second officer braced himself momentarily against a metal cabinet just as a "superflash" jarred the ship to one side, missing them by yards. When he stepped back, he blinked hard, sure he was seeing afterimages. Starkly outlined against the side of the cabinet was a "shadow" of his own hand. Blinking didn't make it go away. Nor was he the only one to see the "lightning phantom" before it began to fade ten minutes later.

ANSWERS:

1. Virtua Fighter 2.
2. Zero.
3. Lightning.
4. A size 8½ (glass) footprint covered in antifreeze.
5. Remedial reading.
6. AB Pizza.
7. Peter.
8. Day-old jelly doughnuts.
9. A picture of Sharon Kiveat (torn from his high school yearbook).
10. Accord, Maxima, or Taurus.

YOUR SCORE _____

Even more up close and personal, lightning figures are the phantom's opposite number, permanent traceries found on the skin of those just too close to the singular power of lightning. A Greek sailor off Zante, struck by lightning, was found with the number 44 imprinted on his skin. He was several feet from the railings with that number and, according to witnesses, never came in contact with the sign on the rail. Considering that a cow struck by lightning in Maryland still carried an image of the robin and its branch when it arrived at the abattoir, maybe someone should have checked out the cows in "D.P.O." more carefully. A single investigator, Professor Poey of Grandiston University, noted some forty instances of lightning figures in his study, including coins, window panes, a lady's fan, a spray of flowers, and, in one delicate situation, a lover's bracelet.

The odd occurrence caused problems for a local priest in Wells, England, back in 1595, when lightning struck the building and dozens of his parishioners found themselves marked with shadows of the altar cross. Superstition rampaged through the village. Some of the marked claimed "special intervention." Those not so marked came under immediate suspicion. If not for the intercession of their bishop, the situation might easily have degenerated into a witch hunt.

"Special" abilities have been claimed by, or attributed to, strike victims long before Darren Oswald was knocked on his keister. In a case eerily reminiscent of Darren's, Catherine Aubigon, an exquisite French courtesan struck by lightning in 1718, set her sights on no less grandiose a lover than her sovereign king.

Since she was the daughter of a prostitute and her transient client, Catherine's prospects seemed even more finite than Darren Oswald's—until, at thirteen, she attracted the eye of Ardon Duchene, a minor nobleman with a taste for young girls who whisked her away from the slums of Arlennes.

Although all-too-worldly in some ways, young Catherine was sadly lacking in experience of things rural. To her, lightning existed only in distant realms above the rooftops. Her ignorance of the connection between trees and rampant electricity was boundless. In the very first spring storm, Catherine, burned across both hands and the sole of one foot, was found way too close to a forty-five-foot cedar.

Fearful servants carried the stunned girl to an elderly parish priest instead of a doctor. Perhaps inspired by his mumbled prayers, or by the vague warding-off gestures of the peasants they passed, Catherine quickly began parlaying beauty, local notoriety, and a burgeoning flair for drama into a new, darker, more dangerously seductive image.

Back in the servants' quarters, a recovering Catherine was suddenly afflicted with visions, prophesying with uncanny accuracy key events in her rapt audience's lives. A boy died. A husband abandoned his wife and eight children. A cook barely escaped the blaze that consumed a summer kitchen. All as Catherine had predicted.

Had her visions remained so tragic, Catherine's career could have led her to a stake instead of to the Parisian court. However, Catherine understood her audience. To the deeply religious peasantry, she professed Divine inspiration, and, with a repertoire of calamity and catastrophe, she quickly included touches of the miraculous. Just as Darren Oswald boasted of having saved his true love's husband, Catherine also "touched" dozens of people on her patron's farms. From children with scraped knees to laboring women, it seemed everyone on the Duchene estate at some time came under the healing "touch," and her "patients" swiftly passed reports of her success through the countryside.

The only one disturbed by Catherine's sudden conversion was Duchene himself. Though his delight in trotting her out to entertain his more prominent friends seemed boundless, he was less pleased when Catherine's near divinity intruded on their bedroom activities and she refused him her favors until a vision moved her to join him. On the one occasion when he attempted to force her door open, metal pots flew from their racks in the kitchen, shutters rattled, and pictures fell from the walls. The burns around the hinges on her door were also new.

Oddly enough, her "visions" began leading her to Duchene's guests' rooms. Perhaps they tipped better. . . .

In any case, it wasn't long before Catherine began to predict her present employer's death. For this bit of information, she was beaten soundly and locked in her room for three days without food or water. When she was let out, she again proclaimed his impending death. He lifted a hand to beat her once more and, on touching her, dropped dead.

After confronting axe-wielding cannibals, liver-munching mutants, and sewage-sucking flukemen, you wouldn't think Scully would balk at a simple human-cum-electric-eel, would you?

The servants later claimed they saw lightning leap from the hands she held up to protect herself.

Far from making her a pariah, the incident propelled her into the realm of a minor celebrity, and within months she'd been installed in the home of a titled gentleman whose interest in the occult was well known. At first, Catherine seemed quite content to advise him on his investments, to do "readings" of the men he was considering doing business with, and to warm his bed during her visions. At least until her uncanny accuracy brought the attention of a wealthy count. When Tampiere refused to let her go with her count, Catherine once again began to foresee death.

Two maids witnessed the final argument. The older one vowed that brilliant light surrounded her employer before he died. The younger one was too busy cringing in a corner to see the light, but she did see the singed lace on Catherine's gloves.

From the count to his first cousin, who happened to live near the

Paris court, and up through the Parisian ranks, Catherine spent three years working her way toward her goal. Somewhere along the way, she began to prophesy the king's ascendancy—with herself at his side. And somewhere along the way, five more men died.

By the time she'd positioned herself in the king's vicinity, Catherine Aubinon had developed an eminence that was remarkable among a sphere of already remarkable people. Her visions continued, coming most accurately at the height of the spring storms. It was during one of these midnight gatherings that Catherine actually came to the attention of the king. Accompanied by his current lady friend, if not his wife, Louis spent considerably more attention on this bizarre woman. While powdered wigs surrounded him, Catherine's wild dark hair flew freely around her shoulders. While the court coquettes fluttered behind their fans, Catherine stalked "her man" openly, deliberately.

For once, however, Catherine's "powers" seemed to fail her—either that, or they weren't up to dealing with the poison that court physicians claimed left her in a back-wrenching rictus by morning. It was many years before the king's bedmate was challenged by an upstart peasant who didn't have enough sense to come in out of the rain.

eXtras:

The X-Files' crew indulges their own taste in music on a fairly regular basis. In addition to the numerous Vandals allusions in this episode, The Rosemarys' video version of "Mary Beth Clark I Love You" made it on-screen.

X

From this episode, we know that Darren was struck by lightning at least four times, either deliberately or accidentally. While that's impressive, it's no record. That belongs to ex-park ranger Ray C. Sullivan of Virginia, who was struck seven times.

Code Name:
"CLYDE BRUCKMAN'S FINAL REPOSE"

CASE SUMMARY:

While investigating the serial slaying of several prognosticators, Scully and Mulder encounter Clyde Bruckman, who seems capable of handing out "eyewitness" accounts of events he's never seen. Scully is about ready to call Bruckman a suspect instead of a witness, but Mulder remains convinced he's found proof of clairvoyance or even predestination.

EYEWITNESS STATEMENT:

"You'll find the woman tomorrow morning. By the fat, little, white, Nazi storm trooper. Glenview Lake. Her body is floating in Glenview Lake. Now, if you'll excuse me, I think I've seen enough deaths for one night."

—Clyde Bruckman

DEEP BACKGROUND:

Peeking into the Future

Humanity's curiosity knows no bounds. As if our pasts and presents weren't filled with enough unanswered questions, we're endlessly fascinated with our own futures. The palmists, tea-leaf readers, and tarotists mentioned in "Clyde Bruckman's Final Repose" are but a few of the divinatory arts' practitioners. While the degree of sophistication varies considerably, not a single culture is completely free of the desire to *know*, or of those people claiming to have the answers. The Scully who finally gives in to Bruckman's temptation is in many ways symbolic of modern society. While we cling to our sciences and technologies, scorning the "old ways," demanding the latest version, we still find horoscopes in all our newspapers.

We might share our predecessors' curiosity, but we'd lose hands down in unearthing innovative ways to satisfy it.

The anthropomancy responsible for those entrails decorating the doll collector's table existed among all major civilizations and religions. There were almost as many forms of the practice as there were animals available for slaughter, though human sacrifice was generally held to give the most accurate readings. From its practice we gained such priceless gems of wisdom as:

- If there are two fingers on the liver, expect rival pretenders to the throne.
- If the lung is red, there will be a conflagration.
- If blood pools in the cavity, a son will be born.

TRIVIA BUSTER 5

Easy Stuff: *A single point for each correct answer.*

1. Why didn't the Stupendous Yappi like Mulder?
2. What does Mrs. Lowell give Bruckman instead of her garbage?
3. Clyde Bruckman described something as a "fat, little, white, Nazi storm trooper." What did Mulder believe it really was?
4. What's Bruckman's tongue-in-cheek suggestion for Mulder's eventual cause of death?
5. What weapon was used to murder the Tarot Reader?

Tougher Trivia: *Two points for each of these stumpers.*

6. What was the palmist's name?
7. What did Clyde Bruckman "give" to Scully?
8. Who did The Stupendous Yappi believe rock star Madonna would become involved with romantically?
9. What pie does Bruckman see in Mulder's future?
10. Where is the palmist's body found?

- If the gallbladder is fat-covered, expect cold weather.
- If the diaphragm clings, the Divine will intervene.

Whether any of these occurrences was favorable or not depended on which side of the body it happened. Anything happening on the right side was a blessing; anything on the left was treated with considerable trepidation. So if the blood predicting the birth of a son were to pool to the right, entire countries might begin celebrating, but if it pooled to the left, the child's parents might well consider drowning it at birth.

Leaves you wondering what configuration of organs and body fluids would translate to "You've just been killed." Perhaps the doll collector ought to have paid closer attention to her tea leaves.

Even that mightn't have helped, though. Things in the X-Filean universe don't always work quite the way they do in ours. Certainly its version of the tarot differs radically from the accepted norm. Even allowing for the "interpretive" nature of the craft, this episode's tarot reading made little sense within the framework of cards shown.

While the Death card is bungled so often in TV and film that audiences would be surprised to see its real meaning, change and transformation, used correctly, *The X-Files* set a high standard for itself in earlier seasons by doing the homework required to avoid the cliché mistakes that leave its well-educated audience groaning. Unfortunately, in this case, the boo-boos didn't stop with a single card.

The Hermit, generally associated with a need to withdraw and re-evaluate life, just doesn't fit the tarotist's interpretation, that the Bell-

ANSWERS:

1. He claimed Mulder gave off "negative energy."
2. Her lighter.
3. A propane tank.
4. Autoerotic asphyxiation.
5. A salad fork.
6. Madam Zelma.
7. A dog.
8. "Superwitness" Kato Kaelin.
9. Banana cream.
10. In Clyde Bruckman's dumpster.

YOUR SCORE _____

hop (or Puppet, as he liked to call himself) was "searching for someone"—much less whether or not his weird client would find anyone.

The Magician, Puppet's second card, seems even more illogical, as it represents everything that Puppet isn't—namely, a master of himself, capable of dealing with problems in a healthy way. With that meaning in mind, the Fortune-Teller's interpretation, that Puppet was seeking a man with special knowledge (presumably Bruckman), is absolutely nonsensical. The Jungian interpretation, that the Seeker is a master of psychic abilities, may be poetically ironic but hardly appropriate, since neither Puppet nor Bruckman could make that claim.

But if there was ever a card least likely to turn up in a reading for Puppet, the Lovers would have to be it. Because it is imbued with the attributes of balance and attraction, and predicts a caring and trusting relationship, there's no possible means to squirm it into this story line. While Scully, "a redhead," would certainly play a role in abruptly ending Pusher's confusion, nothing in the symbolism of the Lovers could have predicted it.

And we won't even mention the sudden addition of a Bellhop to the deck. . . . Or the unlikelihood of turning up a spread with nothing but Major Arcana cards. . . .

Choosing palmists, psychics, and tasseographers as the other victims had a distinct advantage—there's no way to check up on their predictions!

Aleuromancy: After sprinkling flour on oil or water, the Seeker interprets the shapes formed. If, for example, the shape is of a lion's head, a man is possessed by a ghost.

Cleromancy: The casting of lots on a large scale. The Assyrians could cast up to 11,000 dice to distribute the shares of an inheritance or temple income, or to elect officials.

Lecanomancy: Divination by means of a bowl or dish into which oil was poured over water. If the oil divided in two, the Seeker could expect either to go to war or lose a patient. A small drop separating from a larger one forecast a victory or a son's birth.

Libanomancy: By tossing cedar on a brazier and observing the shape and direction of the smoke, a libanomancer tackled everything from capital trials to tomorrow's menu.

Lychnomancy: The notion of Light and Dark, Good and Evil, Knowledge and Ignorance, is so pervasive in human societies that it would have been surprising if some form of divination based on light alone *didn't* arise. Unlike the other forms, however, which depended on direct observations of the organs or dice or smoke, lychnomancy took its cue from the Seeker. After the Seeker had been deprived of light for a considerable period of time, he was brought, blindfolded, into a room filled with brilliant light. The Seeker described in great detail the patterns of light dancing on the insides of his closed eyelids. The shifting patterns should provide whatever answer was needed.

Necromancy: Oddly enough, of the many forms of divination practiced in ancient times, the one that has actually survived the longest, the consultation of the dead, was the most clandestine of the lot, the least likely to enjoy general approval. A Babylonian text relates the tale of the unfortunate Aesirm and Faesher caught attempting to conjure up the spirit of their father. It seems he'd been discourteous enough to die without telling anyone how his lands were to be split. As it turned out, the daughter inherited after her brothers were boiled in oil.

Ornithomancy: Perhaps the most pleasant form of augury, the observation of birds as they flew overhead generally required nothing more than a pleasant hillside to lie on, preferably with a hunk of strong cheese and equally strong wine. A flight of sparrows hovering overhead was a neutral answer to the questions; a flight from the right was a positive response, and a flight from the left a negative.

Plastromancy: Like scapulimancy, plastromancy is an offshoot of anthropomancy. Shells from turtles, tortoises, crabs, or mollusks were read directly from the swirls and ridges, or indirectly from being burned until cracks formed.

Scapulimancy: Reading bones probably began as part of the anthropomancy rituals as just another point to investigate, but quickly split off when practitioners collected odd bone fragments and cast them like lots. In North America, it took a slightly different form. After the slaughter of an animal, whether for general or religious purposes, the scapulae were tossed into a fire, and after cracks had formed, the cracks were read.

eXtras:

Did you catch the joke in Clyde Bruckman's poker hand? Like Wild
Bill Hickok, Bruckman was holding three aces and a pair of eights. It's
been called the Deadman's Hand since it was found in Hickok's hand
on the one occasion when he *didn't* sit with his back to the door—and
got shot.

X

A Brief Filmography of Clyde Bruckman The real Clyde Bruckman,
whom writer Darin Morgan honored in this episode, wrote for the
greats of early film, including the likes of Buster Keaten and W.C.
Fields. Among his scores of projects are:

> *Moon Over Las Vegas*, 1944
> *Half-Shot Shooters*, 1936
> *The Man on the Flying Trapeze*, 1935
> *Leave 'Em Laughing*, 1928
> *Putting Pants on Philip*, 1927
> *Sherlock Jr.*, 1924

X

Remember the "Lolla-whatever" Clyde Bruckman had so much difficulty pronouncing? Well, it's Lollapalooza, an old-style vaudeville performance that has included Jim Rose's troupe. Darin Morgan wrote both "Clyde Bruckman's Final Repose" and "Humbug," which featured Jim Rose's merry band.

Code Name: "THE LIST"

CASE SUMMARY:

"Neech" Manley promised to kill five men—after he died. While prison officials could ignore the rantings of a "prison philosopher" swearing revenge, the growing pile of bodies proves considerably harder to overlook.

EYEWITNESS STATEMENT:

"I will return to avenge all the petty tyranny, and the cruelty I have suffered! I will be recast, reincarnated, reunion of spirit and flesh! Mark my words! Five men will die."

—Neech Manley

Rapidly becoming two of the best known faces on television.

DEEP BACKGROUND:

The Collected Wisdom of Death Row

Given an opportunity for a few "last words," Neech Manley nearly set a new record for most words per minute. He might still be talking if his executioner hadn't finally flipped the switch.

Whether out of morbid curiosity or in the hope of catching some "near-death" wisdom, observers, reporters, and prison staff often find themselves jotting down these final utterances.

Short and Sweet

Unlike Manley, the vast majority of convicts who find themselves offered the chance to leave a few words for posterity keep it short and to the point.

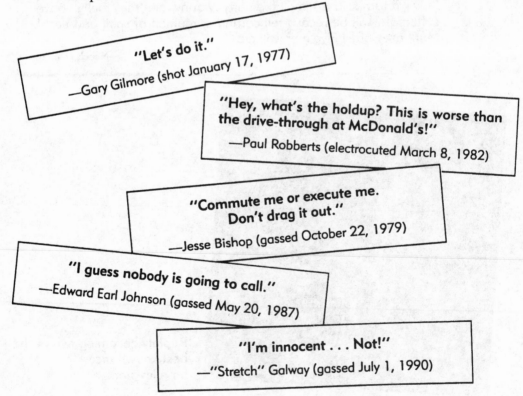

"Let's do it."
—Gary Gilmore (shot January 17, 1977)

"Hey, what's the holdup? This is worse than the drive-through at McDonald's!"
—Paul Robberts (electrocuted March 8, 1982)

"Commute me or execute me. Don't drag it out."
—Jesse Bishop (gassed October 22, 1979)

"I guess nobody is going to call."
—Edward Earl Johnson (gassed May 20, 1987)

"I'm innocent . . . Not!"
—"Stretch" Galway (gassed July 1, 1990)

"You gonna shave me where?!"

—Robert Hurley (electrocuted October 12, 1991)

"Don't you touch that switch, man!
Don't you touch th—"

—Walter Gibson (electrocuted January 12, 1989)

"Yeah, I think I'd rather be fishing."

—Jimmy Glass (electrocuted June 12, 1987)

"I'm sorry."

—Gerald Koss (gassed April 17, 1986)

TRIVIA BUSTER   6

Easy Stuff: *One point for each correct answer.*

1. What was Neech Manley's legal first name?
2. How many people were on Neech's list?
3. For what crime did Neech Manley receive the death penalty?
4. Where did the prisoner work detail find a guard's head?
5. What happened to the warden's car?

Tougher Trivia: *Sharpen a pencil and take two points per answer.*

6. How long had Neech been in jail?
7. What was Neech's prisoner number?
8. What type of bug kept turning up around dead bodies in "The List"?
9. Where was the executioner's body found?
10. How was the guard's head removed?

Taking brevity to the max, James William Hamblen didn't say a word. Instead, he smiled, winked at the onlookers, and then stuck his tongue out at them before the switch was thrown and he was electrocuted on September 21, 1990.

Life After Death

An amazing number of those facing execution find some form of religion, and as Scully said, "Reincarnation has always been popular on death row—for obvious reasons." Religious convictions, condemnations, and attempts at renewed negotiations have all found their way into those final speeches.

> "I forgive you all, for you know not what you do."
>
> —Samein Straub, to observers (injected May 3, 1993)

> "Oh, well, a bug ain't so bad. How could I screw that up?"
>
> —Jerry Lloyd (hung February 19, 1992)

ANSWERS:

1. Napoleon.
2. Five.
3. For driving the getaway car in a double homicide.
4. In a paint can.
5. It slammed into a tree—with the warden at the wheel.
6. Eleven years, fifty-six days.
7. 50416.
8. The greenbottle fly and its larvae.
9. In his own attic.
10. With a putty knife.

YOUR SCORE _____

"Da phone is gonna ring. I did my novenas."
—William Atwater (injected April 22, 1989)

"Guess I shouldn'ta killed that nun, heh?"
—Paul Tighe (hung March 2, 1990)

"Only good thing about dying is I get another shot at you."
—Raymond M. Carver, to his mother
(hung August 6, 1990)

Prison Poets

A few of those condemned to death took a more artistic view of the whole thing, obviously conscious of the pencils scribbling across notebooks.

"You can be a king or a street sweeper,
but everybody dances with the Grim Reaper."

—Robert Alton Harris (gassed April 21, 1992)

"Roses are red, violets are blue,
I got Bobby, and I'm gonna get you!"

—Tommy Lee Guthrie (electrocuted May 11, 1990)

"Do not go gentle into that good night!
Bitch, bitch, bitch against the coming of the dark!"

—Enrico Nuevo (gassed November 10, 1987)

Last, but Not Least

The record for the longest set of last words undoubtedly belongs to Hubert Muthison, who, before being electrocuted in January of 1984, recited, word for word, three-quarters of the Book of Revelations. He might have finished if the executioner's hand hadn't fallen asleep during the presentation and accidentally depressed the switch.

For original material though, Calvin "Coolio" Cooper, who eventually died from lethal injection, would be hard to top.

> "I made my confession to the priest you sent me, now I gonna make confession for them what sinned against *me*! You know who you are. You know what I mean. I didn't do nothing alone. . . .
>
> "And that lawyer, yeah, right, I'd a done better to defend myself! Your time is coming, man, you'll see. If'n I don' get back for you next time around, some fool will get hisself off in *spite* of you and then you'll be screwed right. . . ."

Sound familiar? How about:

> "I can count you off, a whole handful of you! Might take me a while, but I *am* comin' back, and I won't be waitin' for no judges, no evidence, no prissy lawyers to tell me what you got comin'!"

Calvin, however, doesn't seem to have been nearly as successful in his attempt at reincarnation; none of the people on his personal hit list have come to any harm.

Over three seasons, the writers have created some memorable monologues for the leads and the recurring characters. For pure power of presentation, however, the soliloquy created for Neech Manley remains difficult to top.

eXtras:

Meanwhile . . . Back on Death Row Capital punishment, one of a very few issues capable of sinking or saving a politician's career, is also one of the few concerns where hard numbers are available. So when *The*

X-Files drew some fire for its lack of white inmates, it didn't take long to number-crunch reality and compare it to TV-land.

Of the 3,009 people on death row in the spring of 1995, 48 percent (1,443), and by far the largest group, were white. Unlike *The X-Files'* all-black cast of convicts, national statistics indicate that only 40 percent (1,204) of defendants are black. Two hundred thirty-three Latinos, 52 Native Americans, 22 Asians, and 30 people of unspecified descent round out the remaining 12 percent.

However, in most areas, X-Filean figures are in line with those issued each year by the federal government. With an average death row stay of *seven and a half* years, most residents have lots of time to ponder their lifestyles, debate philosophy, or even invent their own religion. And, oddly enough, sanctioned execution is one of the least common ways for inmates to leave The Block. Since 1973, 1,458 convictions and/or sentences were reversed, 90 died either of natural causes or at the hands of their fellow inmates, 72 sentences were commuted, and 42 convicts committed suicide. Only 288 men and a single woman have actually been executed. Being black doesn't seem to affect a defendant's chances after hitting death row either. Whites accounted for 55 percent of those actually executed; blacks, only 39 percent.

While the population in *The X-Files'* version of death row wasn't exactly representative, Florida certainly was the ideal setting for "The List." Only Texas has executed more prisoners.

X

A Philosophical Approach It's not the sort of thing most people think about, but death row inmates aren't "most people," and the percentage of waking thought they've given over to contemplating capital punishment's immediate, physical results isn't just higher than that of the general population, but considerably more intimate.

When Bill Boggs, awaiting execution by electrocution for his seven murders, discovered that his cellmate, Jeffrey Crain, was due to die by the same means only months earlier, Boggs saw this as the perfect opportunity to satisfy his own morbid curiosity. Since Crain was permitted to ask three people to witness his execution, but hadn't yet put together his "guest list," Boggs traded six packs of cigarettes for the privilege of peering in through the glass window.

Seven months after Crain's death, Boggs's journals continued to reflect the profound impact the experience had on him.

"Living with a man in an eight by ten cage for months, you'd think you'd already smelled just about every smell he could produce, but you'd be wrong. Even through the glass I smelled him. That stench climbed right up my nose. Soap don't get rid of it either. It got into my hair, sometimes I swear I can still smell it. The warden must reek of it."

While it's likely the smell of burned skin and hair that haunted Boggs was more psychological than physical, his other entries prove he was paying close attention. In over 560 pages of his thirty-three journals, he describes the stark reality of death by electrocution; how a man's eyes stare out, fixed on the last thing he sees as the heat cooks them a milky white; how the gel at his temples sizzles; and how the witnesses of Crain's death heard bones snap while his body, taut with the energy racing through it, arched against the restraints. Most horrifying for Boggs, however, was his unshakable conviction that Crain, despite the electricity supposedly scrambling any messages to his brain, lived long enough to experience every insult inflicted on him.

"Even as his eyes were cooking, he was still looking out at me with knowing."

Boggs never did get to find out what it was like firsthand. Before his own execution, death by lethal injection replaced electrocution. On the day he heard that the prison's chair had finally been removed, replaced with gurneys and IV racks, he curled into a ball in the center of his bunk and wept like a child for hours. The following morning, he declared himself a born-again Christian, who thanked God for answering the prayers of even "the least deserving of his children."

X

Like "Duane Barry" from season two, "The List" was directed by Chris Carter himself; unlike "Duane Barry," this episode is seldom cited as one of an X-Phile's top ten.

Code Name: "2SHY"

CASE SUMMARY:

A serial killer with unusual tastes is using the Internet as his hunting ground—and complicating Scully and Mulder's investigations by making it nearly impossible to identify his victims.

EYEWITNESS STATEMENT:

"Yes, scorpions predigest their food outside of their bodies by regurgitating onto their prey, but . . . I don't know too many scorpions who surf the Internet."

—Special Agent Dana Scully

DEEP BACKGROUND:

Odd Tastes

Serial killers, at least the fictional variety, remain among the public's pet villains, so it's hardly surprising that our favorite agents spend so much time tracking them. And with the enduring popularity of character Eugene Victor Tooms—after nearly seventy episodes, still the only repeat villain—it was just a matter of scheduling before Mulder and Scully ran into yet another serial killer with a taste for humanity. Considering the variety of methods and motives already used by real-life cannibal killers, it's amazing the X-crew could find *anything* these crazy culinary connoisseurs hadn't already tried!

Like the American King of Cannibals, Jeffrey Dahmer, 2SHY evidently considered humans an important chunk of his diet. Dahmer, however, probably didn't lure his victims into fancy French restau-

rants. When he was arrested, Dahmer's weight so alarmed prison officials that they immediately increased his caloric intake. Determining
his favorite dishes did take some time, though, and peeking into his
fridge wasn't much help. Other than some condiments, it was completely empty. Perhaps 2SHY did see Dahmer as something of a mentor, though. Like 2SHY, Dahmer disposed of the bodies by allowing
them to dissolve in an acid bath. 2SHY just cut out the middle man by
providing his own acid.

Had 2SHY met up with Russia's Andrei Chikatilo, the two might
even now have been happily cohabiting in the nearest pumpkin shell.
Like Dahmer, Chikatilo was skeletal when he was finally run to
ground. With over fifty confirmed kills and nearly a hundred more
suspected, Chikatilo's larder was seldom empty, but, as a true modern
man, fat repulsed him. After sautéing his victims, mostly children,
Chikatilo skimmed off the fat 2SHY so desperately wanted and sold it
to farmers to mix with their animal feed.

Of course, if 2SHY had lived in Hanover in 1924, he might have
discovered a vendor carrying *exactly* what he was looking for and practically eliminated any risk of exposure! So successful were lovers Fritz

TRIVIA BUSTER   7

Easy Stuff: *One point for each correct answer.*

1. What charm did Lauren MacKalvey wear during her last date?
2. What was Ellen Kaminsky's on-line name?
3. In what chat room did Lauren MacKalvey and Virgil Incanto meet?
4. What did Incanto's landlady want him to read?
5. What did Jesse think Incanto smelled like?

Tougher Trivia: *Get these and you'll earn your two points.*

6. One of Virgil Incanto's on-line names was 2SHY. What was the other?
7. What was "missing" from the remains of the victims?
8. At what restaurant was Ellen to meet Incanto?
9. What was Incanto's writing specialty?
10. What charm is attached to Ellen's key chain?

An outdoor shoot during the filming of "2SHY" reveals the secret of Anderson's ever-changing height.

Haarmann and Hans Grans at stalking young boys that they started their own profitable sideline. In addition to the amazingly eclectic collection of children's clothes and toys the pair sold, they supplied a local butcher with "unusually spiced" smoked meats.

As disgusting as Haarmann and Grans's crimes seem, even they weren't particularly original as cannibals go. Only a few years before, in Düsseldorf, Georg Grossman was supplementing the stores in his own shop with the horrific "scraps" from his table. The tally of his victims could never be proved, but even during his trial he couldn't seem to locate the receipts for the raw meat in approximately *two tons* of "beef and pork sausages" sold from his shop. He might have continued indefinitely had police not responded to a disturbing-the-peace call and found the neatly skinned and butchered carcasses of three women hanging to age and a fourth dead girl about to undergo the same process. The choice bits of all the victims, including those of the fourth woman—who'd shared his bed the previous night—were found in Grossman's icebox.

Or maybe 2SHY should have teamed up with Henry Lee Lucas. . . . When Otis Toole became the sadist's partner in crime and expressed his liking for human barbecue ribs, Lucas was happy to help Toole hunt. Then, to Toole's delight, Lucas professed an extreme dislike for rib sauce! While they were content to share in the deaths of some two hundred women, Lucas's interest in dead women was considerably more carnal. A partnership made in heaven.

Frankly, for pure physical depravity, *nothing* fictional approaches the inventiveness of history's real-life cannibals—not even *The X-Files*. Luckily for these consummate storytellers, easy shocks are seldom the first choice. Instead, drawing on the psychological horror they produce with such eerie authenticity that their presentation can appear effortless, they created a cannibal who feeds on the soul as well as the flesh.

"2SHY" might have been a trip back to the story well, just another medical mutant with an insatiable hunger for something human, but unlike either "Tooms" or "Squeeze," or even "3," which introduced audiences to a bloodthirsty trio, "2SHY" took us to the depths of *human* evil. Whatever strange craving consumed this killer was secondary to the cruel game he *chose* to play with his victims.

Getting On-Line

When *The X-Files* chose to follow the media pack with this episode, jumping on the "evil Internet" theme, many X-Philes were more than a bit surprised. They expected an intriguing twist on a hackneyed story line, but received instead another stereotypical depiction of cybernauts as relationship-impaired and the 'Net as a meeting place for sexual deviants. Considering the tremendous support the program has received from the on-line community, fans could be forgiven for expecting a slightly more enlightened effort.

ANSWERS:

1. A four-leaf clover.
2. Huggs.
3. Big & Beautiful.
4. Her poems, a lot of her poems.
5. Dish soap.
6. Timid.
7. Adipose, fatty tissue.
8. Les Trois Étoiles, The Three Stars.
9. The translation of obscure Italian poetry.
10. A rabbit's foot.

YOUR SCORE _____

The show itself spawned some 100-plus Web sites in less than three years, including an official site operated by Fox Television (http://www.TheX-Files/com/), and dozens of equally well done fan-sponsored sites. The World Wide Web pages really do encompass the globe with sites, both English- and foreign-language, in Norway (http://bundy.hibo.no/~Larsen/x-files/x-files.html), Italy (http://www.cs.unibo.it/~cobianch/index.html), Singapore (http://www.iscs.nus.sg/~chenmin/xfiles/xf.html), Australia (http://www.cs.mu.ox.au/~simc/xfiles.html), Brazil (http://www.iis.com.br/~lpaulo/xfiles.html), Ireland (http://www.eeng.dcu.ie/~stdcu/x-files/x-files.html) and the United Kingdom (http://www.zynet.co.uk/simon/x-files/), among other countries.

For those with slightly more primitive Internet access, the File Transfer Protocol (FTP) can still net you text-based articles, pictures, sound bytes, even movie clips to play on your home computer. Try ftp.u.washington.edu/public/roland/x-files or ftp.cs.nmt.edu/xfiles.

If you just can't get enough X-Philean discussion over the water cooler on Monday morning, there are dozens of on-line connections to other 'Philes, everything from electronic mailing lists to Usenet groups to real-time discussion areas on #xf and #xfiles on the Internet Relay Chat (IRC). From the ludicrous to the critical, X-Philes easily find conversations suited to their interest level and personalities. The major on-line services all provide their customers with forums and chat areas as well, including Compuserve, America On-Line, Genie, and Delphi, which is a corporate cousin to Fox and hosts its own "official" discussion areas while offering an "exclusive" line of merchandising products.

For the fan who just can't get enough of David Duchovny, Gillian Anderson, Mitch Pileggi—or their favorite villains—there are WWW, FTP, and mailing lists devoted to the actors as well as the characters they portray.

On-Line Mailing Lists:

North American Mail List: Mail to majordomo@chaos.taylored.com with "subscribe X-FILES" as your message.

United Kingdom Mail List: Mail to listproc@uel.ac.uk with "subscribe X-FILES" as your message.

German Mail List: Mail to listserv@stargate.pfalz.de with "subscribe xf-de" as your message.

Usenet Newsgroups:

alt.tv.x-files	North American discussion group
alt.tv.x-files.creative	Fan fiction based on *The X-Files*
uk.media.tv.sf.x-files	United Kingdom discussion group
aus.tv.x-files	Australian discussion group
alt.binaries.x-files	Images, sounds, movies, screen-savers

eXtras:

As in past episodes, the writers continue adding layers of meaning with everything at their disposal, including character names. Take Virgil Incanto . . .

"Incanto," aside from the name's obvious poetic allusion, shares roots in the words "enchantment," "fascination," and "incantation," all appropriate in light of the character's ability to find "just what to say."

Poetry comes up again with "Virgil," who, in addition to being a famous Roman poet, is the guide of *The Divine Comedy* (which is also written in cantos) through Dante's version of hell, a place this Virgil Incanto appeared all too willing to lead his hapless victims.

X

I morti non sono piu soli . . . The dead are no longer lonely.

X

Who's Who in the FBI This episode isn't the first to raise the issue of chauvinism in the ranks of law enforcement. In "Soft Light," Scully makes a point of telling her partner that being a woman in the FBI is still a difficult career choice. Though women have joined the real world's FBI ranks, they still number only 1,359 of the more than 10,000 in service. See Tables 1 and 2.

Table 1
EMPLOYEE STATISTICS

Special Agent Employment Statistics as of 11/1/95:

	Number of Men	Percent of Total	Number of Women	Percent of Total	Total Group	Percent of Total
Amer. Indian	42	.4	6	.1	48	.5
Asian	163	1.6	16	.2	179	1.8
Black	466	4.6	93	.9	559	5.5
Hispanic	596	5.9	66	.6	662	6.5
White	7532	74.1	1178	11.6	8710	85.7
Totals	8799	86.6	1359	13.4	10158	100
All Minorities	1267	12.5	181	1.8	1448	14.3

Table 2

Support Personnel Employment Statistics as of 11/1/95:

	Number of Men	Percent of Total	Number of Women	Percent of Total	Total Group	Percent of Total
Amer. Indian	17	.1	36	.3	53	.4
Asian	98	.7	126	.9	224	1.6
Black	643	4.7	3112	22.7	3755	27.4
Hispanic	159	1.2	411	3.0	570	4.2
White	3097	22.6	6012	43.8	9109	66.4
Totals	4014	29.3	9697	70.7	13711	100
All Minorities	917	6.7	3685	26.9	4602	36.6

X

 Blooper Alert! Okay, you've got to dig a bit for this one, but . . . Castiglione's *Il Libro del Cortegiano* isn't a book of poetry. A collection of essays in debate form, *Il Libro del Cortegiano* (The Book of the Courtier), is actually a Renaissance How-To, a sort of Emily Post of how to behave at court. While it has a section on *how* to write poetry for your current *amore*, it doesn't give any examples.

Incidentally, *La Vita Nuova* wasn't written by anyone named Ginicelli either, but by Dante Alighieri. Unlike *Il Libro del Cortegiano*, a sixteenth-century volume, *La Vita Nuova* was penned in the thirteenth, rather a large spread even for the Italian Renaissance. Neither text is particularly obscure.

Code Name: "THE WALK"

CASE SUMMARY:

One soldier has already killed himself, and another is desperately try-ing to duplicate that feat when Mulder arrives already convinced that a "phantom soldier" is at work.

Scully's more traditional theories quickly lead them to the killer's accomplice, but seem to have failed when the supposed killer himself turns out to be a quadruple amputee.

EYEWITNESS STATEMENT:

". . . what I can't figure out is why a man who so deliberately and methodically set out to commit suicide would leave the one en-trance to the room unsecured. But then again, I obviously have a feeble grasp of Army protocol and procedure."

—Special Agent Fox Mulder

DEEP BACKGROUND:

Out of Body or Out of Mind?

In addition to convincing performances, a subtle mastery of light and sound, and quality cinematography, *The X-Files* is blessed with some of the most talented of today's television writers.

Some shows content themselves with the latest disease of the week; *The X-Files* tackles tomorrow's possibilities. A simple, linear plot— even one interspersed with the bouncing bods of bodacious babes—

simply can't carry the tangled twists of coincidence and conspiracy that X-Philes demand. And while shock value keeps more than a few current programs afloat, *The X-Files* took *storytelling* to a new level when audiences found the sorry state of Elder Care and the plight of war vets as shocking as any alien or monster.

Watching *The X-Files*, you can't help but be struck by its internal consistency. Whether within the frame of each episode or as part of an entire season, its multitude of plotlines work together to create a wonderfully seamless illusion of reality.

Details—like reprising the same actor as a lobby guard in several episodes—count. So do the threads of authenticity constantly being worked into story lines, dialogue, and settings. Allusions to the O.J. trial and Bart Simpson set each show firmly in our reality regardless of their otherworldliness. *Everything* in an episode of *The X-Files* matters, and "The Walk" was no exception. Somehow, GIs, Kirlian photography, remote viewing, suicide, a "phantom" limb pain, the tight community formed by the military, and some astral projection combined for an eerie, atmospheric thriller.

From Scene One of "The Walk," *The X-Files* created a haunting setting from the all-too-real lives of disabled veterans. Characters, situations, and key relationships were painted with quick, deft strokes. Convincing an audience that a character like Rappo, so filled with hate, so thirsty for vengeance, could exist was easy, with the small, daily horrors of his life already portrayed so vividly on-screen. From there to a madman capable of striding across astral planes to reach his victims seems a very small step. With just a few touches of the paranormal brush, we were taken from haunted to terrified.

With popular smashes like *Ghost* making genre limits meaningless, even the "uninitiated," the staunch nonbeliever, recognizes the common elements of near-death experiences, astral projection, and out-of-body dreaming. First there's a dreaming state, then the feeling of disassociation from the physical world, a brief floating sensation, even briefer glimpses of the deserted body below, then flight across a plane where time and distance have little or no meaning. *The X-Files*, however, picked a more subtle detail, the idealized form of that astral body, and made it an integral plot point, the thematic key to all the other elements.

It was experimentation on disfigured leaves that first gave researchers the idea that humans, in fact literally everything, had an "invisible body." Though the mechanism was seldom explained to the satisfaction of more conventional scientists, the electromagnetic signature of a whole leaf, captured on X-ray film, was identical to the outline generated by any part of the leaf. Missing digits from hands and feet created the same ghostly glow as their remaining mates. The "aura" psychics claimed hovered about each of us might actually be quantifiable! Early observations of the Kirlian effect, named for the Soviet scientists who publicized the phenomenon, appeared to support that contention. Timed exposures of leaves separated from their parent plants showed a gradual, but distinct, decline in electromagnetic "energy." Rocks, pennies, and buttons displayed only a consistent, less energetic pattern.

It didn't take long to link these rainbow images to everything from psychic healing to out-of-body experiences to phantom limb pain and the *chi* of the Eastern philosophies. As if to prove that the aura around

TRIVIA BUSTER 8

Easy Stuff: *Take a point for each correct answer.*

1. What odd item did Mulder carry around the base?
2. How did Captain Draper, the general's adjutant, die?
3. What was stolen from General Callahan's home?
4. What toys were Trevor Callahan's passion?
5. What insect had infested Quinton "Roach" Freely's apartment?

Tougher Trivia: *These earn two well-deserved points each.*

6. Lieutenant Colonel Stans wasn't the only one who was inventive in his suicide attempts. How did Staff Sergeant Kevin Aikland kill himself?
7. Where did Trevor Callahan die?
8. What was Rappo's "physical challenge"?
9. What was the unusual cause of death for Roach Freely?
10. How did Mulder decipher the message on the general's answering machine?

a human was essentially different from that of a coin or a leaf, psychics discovered patterns suggesting people could manipulate their electromagnetic fields. Colors shimmered in the blues and purples as psychics "rested" with their hands on the film; they spiked into oranges, lurid greens, and brilliant reds as the subjects brought their "abilities" to bear. Even those with no previous ability could, through biofeedback techniques, train themselves to affect the patterns left on the film. Of course, once results began to appear "repeatable," practicality reared its head and researchers were prodded to find some use for their discovery.

By putting patients in touch with this invisible part of their bodies, the same techniques promised relief from "phantom limb pain." Learning to avoid stubbing one's psychic toes didn't alleviate every patient's pain, but it did work for a remarkable number. At a time when acupuncture and acupressure began impressing Western physicians, the biofeedback-Kirlian combination was received with less skepticism than might otherwise have been the case and found its way into the popular media as well as widely read medical journals. Its similarity to self-hypnosis, however, eventually left it in the realm of "alternative" medicine. While Lamaze later emerged as accepted practice and "positive imagery" found its way into fields like psychology and sports medicine, the Kirlian work languished until New Age alternatives became popular once again. When *The X-Files'* Mulder wandered about with his frames of dental film, it reflected a more modern,

ANSWERS:

1. Film for dental X-rays.
2. She was drowned.
3. Mail.
4. A set of toy soldiers.
5. Ants.
6. He threw himself into a wood-chipper.
7. In his sandbox.
8. He was a quadruple amputee.
9. He died of suffocation after having a bedsheet shoved down his throat—in a solitary cell.
10. Suspecting backward-masking, he played it in reverse.

YOUR SCORE _____

For a man once dubbed as "the actor most likely
to forget to act," Duchovny crams tons of "emoting"
into glances like this.

if equally curious, use that some have found for Kirlian images—ghost
hunting.

The idea of a living ghost, however, was an X-Filean twist that
didn't only hark back to the old notion of what an aura might be, but
drew in parapsychology's kissing cousin, remote viewing. Most of us

prefer to believe we're more than a bunch of cells, that part of us survives physical death. Few of us, however, envision a purpose for that "soul" until death. Remote viewing challenges that idea. Taking the often accidental out-of-body experience to the next level, combining it with a conscious degree of self-hypnosis, supposedly allows the practitioner not only to float about randomly, incorporating an astral stroll into his dreams, but *direct* the astral self to specific places, even times.

In 1975, a series of tests began in and around the San Francisco area. Dozens of men and women, each with a map in a sealed envelope tucked under their pillows, drifted off to sleep. In the morning, tape whirred, recording everything the subjects could remember "seeing" during the night while technicians collected the envelopes. Obvious "misses" received breakfast and a ride home. For those whose accounts appeared to match the unknown location under their pillows, it was the beginning of a week of new, unorthodox ideas and bizarre naps.

Hooked up to an EEG so they could be awakened as soon as their dream state ended, and before they could forget those "dreams," seven women and four men matched ten or more "unique and significant" points from their dreams to locations still sealed away from them. Those eleven took three days to return to their normal sleep schedules, then sat down with a series of photos, matching dream to reality. Of the seven locations given to each participant, seventy-seven in all, only three were mismatched.

To that point, both subjects and researchers had proceeded on the assumption that some unconscious, or more accurately subconscious, process was at work. The "psychic" influence was still considered an essential prerequisite; the question had always been couched in terms of "given an unknown target." What if these eleven people were given a *known* target to view?

Like Rappo, who admittedly obtained his information a little more flamboyantly, each of the eleven subjects was tucked in bed with a definite destination in mind. At those destinations, eleven volunteers began eleven unusual activities. For four hours, in brilliantly colored outfits, they danced, juggled, played a variety of musical instruments—almost anything that should stand out in even a dreamer's mind. The next morning, nine of the eleven were able to pick their volunteers' pictures from the scrapbook, seven identified the activity (even down to the unicyclist who toppled off and bruised his left elbow), and one went as far as to match not only his own volunteer and activity, but those of two other subjects as well!

The next step seemed obvious. Develop a setup to determine if the successful subjects could become more than passive observers. Was it possible for an astral projection to act on the physical world? According to the San Francisco group, which developed four different testing scenarios, no.

For the fictional characters of *The X-Files*, that wasn't a problem, and thanks to the program's careful weaving of probable, possible, and impossible, its audience was equally free to ignore reality for forty-seven minutes and get taken along for a bone-shakingly frightening ride.

eXtras:

Though Rappo wasn't a probable candidate for an Arlington burial, with the prestigious cemetery nearly at capacity, it's unlikely he would have been buried there anyway.

X

Wondering how Ian Tracey, the actor playing Leonard "Rappo" Trimble, became so convincing a quadruple amputee? Toby Lindala created prosthetic stumps, including the "bleeding" left arm, while cunningly hiding Tracey's real limbs in mattresses and wheelchairs.

X

To create the illusion of a second "person" in the pool, Nancy Sorel, who portrayed Capt. Janet Draper, was pulled backward through the water in a harness which was later erased digitally. The various shadowy figures jumping out of sandboxes, steam, and chlorinated pools were created in reverse, by adding a model "painted" with the appropriate surface.

X

Blooper Alert! Either Scully is illustrating her background as a "Navy brat," or the X-crew just doesn't realize that a lieutenant colonel in the *Army* is called "Colonel" or "Sir," but *never* "Lieutenant Colonel."

Code Name: "OUBLIETTE"

CASE SUMMARY:

When Mulder's theories and the forensic evidence conflict, he finds himself at odds with not only his partner and local law enforcement, but also the woman he's trying to defend. To recover another young woman, he'll have to teach his partner to believe in something completely unquantifiable, and a previous victim to believe in herself.

EYEWITNESS STATEMENT:

"I've probably experienced just about everything once or twice. It's all been pretty temporary."

—Lucy Householder

DEEP BACKGROUND:

The Ultimate Long-Distance Plan

"I don't know how to explain it, but I think that Wade's abduction of Amy triggered some kind of . . . physical response in Lucy. Some kind of empathic transference—"

—Special Agent Fox Mulder

Luckily for forensic investigators, no one's yet managed to bleed any blood other than his own—much as some may have wished they could. Empathic transference, in a variety of forms, however, has been reported by many witnesses and is well documented in several cases.

Carol and Karen Dubrosky, twin sisters from Montreal, presented a startling case in 1984. Admitted to a local emergency room at 5:21 P.M., after losing an encounter with a deep fryer, Carol had second-degree burns that covered most of her left hand and forearm. As Carol was being treated, Karen's shocked husband was leaving a message on his in-laws' machine: "Listen, I'm at the hospital with Karen. No one's sure what's wrong yet. . . ." Records from the other hospital prove Karen was admitted at 5:27 P.M. With "spontaneously appearing" burns and several "open and weeping blisters" across the surface of her "left hand and forearm." Though Karen's "injuries" faded within hours, her doctors remained dissatisfied with their own theory, that Karen displayed an extreme reaction to a contact allergen. What in her home hadn't she already handled dozens of times? Nothing.

Less dramatic but equally revealing is the wartime story of Private Randell Foster. Though he was never far from his worried mother's thoughts, on January 14, 1943, Chloe Foster took a break from her normal chores to write in her journal: "All morning, I've been wracked with chills. My hands and feet are so cold I can barely feel my toes." The entry continues, detailing a "dream" of the night before: "I was

TRIVIA BUSTER 9

Easy Stuff: *Take a point for each correct answer.*

1. What did the Tow Truck Driver try to fix for Wade?
2. Where did Wade keep his victims?
3. What confusing evidence was found on Lucy Householder's uniform?
4. What was Lucy Householder's cause of death?
5. From what odd condition was Lucy Householder suffering when she arrived at the hospital?

Tougher Trivia: *Two points for each correct answer.*

6. What school did Amy Jacobs attend?
7. Name the photography company Wade worked for.
8. Where did Lucy Householder live?
9. Where was Lucy Householder found after her abduction?
10. What was Amy's mother's name?

Guest performances like those by Jewel Staite have helped propel
***The X-Files* to the top of a competitive heap.**

under the ice, looking up, seeing soldiers through it. I was drowning, I'm sure." A few weeks later, the War Department notified Mrs. Foster that her son would be home on February 26. Randell Foster had been swept under the ice while crossing a frozen river. The four toes he lost to frostbite after being rescued by his unit made him unfit for further duty. He had fallen through on January 13, 1943.

Such incidents among family members are, relatively speaking, common. Less frequent are events like that of the fictional Amy and Lucy, who apparently were complete strangers. As reporting a *shared* experience is rather difficult if neither person knows who the other might be, it's hardly surprising that none are reported, but many instances of "empathy" have nothing to do with blood ties.

Kelly White, a CPA, and Hannah Lowell, an office manager, worked for the same company, shared the same bench for lunch, and ran together twice a week. Other than friendship, nothing linked the two until October 2, 1994. Hannah skipped the usual Saturday-afternoon run to attend a wedding. At 3:47, Kelly was knocked thirty-two feet from the side of the road by a hit-and-run driver. Hannah, gasping with pain, had to be led out of the church before the ceremony began at 4:00—and insisted someone contact the police, that she was sure something had happened to Kelly. A passerby had seen the collision. The call came in to the Detroit police on the heels of the eyewitness report. Hannah, completely recovered, arrived at the hospital just minutes after the ambulance to identify her battered friend.

Peter St. Jean never met Gregory Barstowe until *after* what he described as a "waking dream." While sitting at his desk in Hampton Court, St. Jean heard someone call out, "Greg! Look out!" He was shocked to feel the glass window behind his office chair shatter. Assuming the shout had been a warning to someone on the street outside, and that the glass had been hit by a ball or something, Peter St. Jean dove under his desk to avoid the shards falling around him. Checking himself from that area of safety, he "saw" a long, jagged cut extending from his elbow to his little finger. Outside, he could still "hear" someone screaming, "Greg! Greg!" Carefully avoiding the glass all over the floor, he crawled back out and hurried toward the window to see who else might be injured outside—and ran smack into an intact pane of glass!

In his own words: "I looked out the window, realizing it couldn't really have broken, but still 'seeing' blood running down my arm and the glitter of broken glass all around me. It was as if there were two fields of view, one atop the other. Outside, I 'saw' a woman just below the window, pressing down on a deep cut in 'Greg's' thigh. She was crying and screaming for help. Then it was gone. Nothing. They simply disappeared."

When he turned back, the room appeared perfectly normal. There

---

ANSWERS:

1. A flat tire, a blown sidewall.
2. In a basement.
3. Amy Jacobs's blood.
4. She drowned—in the backseat of a police car.
5. Glossolalia, incoherent speech.
6. Valley Woods High School, Seattle, WA.
7. Larken Photography.
8. Bright Angel Halfway House.
9. Easton.
10. Myra Jacobs.

YOUR SCORE _____

was no gashed arm, no glass on the floor. His wife, however, was staring at him as if he'd gone mad.

It took him nearly an hour to reorient himself and explain why he'd been crawling about on all fours. So intense had the experience been, Peter St. Jean was convinced he'd suffered a brief psychotic episode. But once she'd heard the story, his wife wasn't so sure. While not a "believer" per se, she'd seen a television documentary about attempts to debunk claims of the paranormal and was disturbed by the similarity Peter's story shared with one of those chronicled. Thinking the house, newly bought, might be "haunted," she called a friend at a local paper and asked if maybe something similar had happened at their address in the past.

There was no such record, but while the reporter was checking the archives, a co-worker called in a human interest story. A Gregory Barstowe had just then survived surgery to repair a leg nearly cut off by glass falling from a broken window. The story continued: "If not for the swift action of Mr. Barstowe's companion, who held the wound together and applied pressure to the severed artery, surgeons say they would never have had the opportunity to save the man or the leg."

The following day, St. Jean and his wife stopped by the hospital, where St. Jean easily picked out Gregory Barstowe from the general ward and immediately recognized his "companion," who was using a pay phone in the hallway. Jill Parker, the companion, was swathed in gauze from her wrist to her elbow. The same falling glass had sliced open her arm.

What separates these accounts from the realm of simple telepathy is their immediacy. Hannah swore she "tasted" blood on the back of her tongue. All those mentioned here felt something of the pain of the "other" member of these strange events. All of their senses tuned in to the experience. For those brief moments, they weren't mere observers but, in some way, participants in the events being played out. Randell Foster's mother didn't "see" her son fall into the water; she *shared* his terror, and his viewpoint, from below the ice.

Obviously, none of the physical laws we currently embrace explain these odd events. The timing alone seems to make such tales implausible. Yet in each of these cases, independent observers confirmed the time lines. Few of those involved had any prior interest in the paranormal. Most of them were terrified by the experience. All of them were delighted to be "one-shot wonders." Not one wanted to "see," "hear," or "feel" anything like it again.

In fact, this empathic transference does seem to be a once-in-a-lifetime event. Of the many reports detailed each year, only a very few are "repeaters" in the Lucy-Amy model used in "Oubliette."

Twins Peter and Paul Harvey, almost unique in the ongoing nature of their experiences, have reported odd happenings since they were three years old. Peter stepped on a nail in the yard; Paul yelled and grabbed his foot in the kitchen. Paul broke an arm in gym class; Peter clutched his own arm and threw up in the middle of his English Lit. lecture. Bee stings, mumps, Paul's first hangover . . . It seems the two could have no secrets from each other. Though the disconcerting incidents trailed off as the two grew older, Paul's wife credits this strange relationship with saving her husband's life. During a family barbecue, Peter, who wasn't even eating, gasped loudly once, then began to turn a faint shade of blue. Looking around and failing to see her husband anywhere, Janet Harvey hurried into the backyard. Paul, perched on a lawn chair, had been watching the coals while finishing off a burger when he'd inhaled a fragment of bread.

Neither of the Harvey twins is extraordinary individually. They don't score high on psi tests. The craps table is as cruel to them as to anyone else. Despite numerous attempts to re-create this odd form of communication, they've been completely unsuccessful.

eXtras:

Details matter! Catch the musical addition at the end of this episode? Commonly called a Kyrie, those soaring tones are part of most requiem masses. *Kyrie Eleison, Christe eleison*: Lord, have mercy.

X

This episode struck a tad too close to home for some viewers, echoing many of the real-life incidents connected with the Polly Klaas abduction in northern California. Like the fictional Amy, Polly was taken from her own room as her sister watched. Richard Davis, like the Carl Wade who sprang from the imagination of *The X-Files'* crew, carried his victim in the trunk of his car. Like Wade, Davis ran into unexpected company while transporting the child. Wade met up with an enterprising tow truck driver after blowing a tire; Davis was stopped by the police for a violation. Tragically, unlike Amy, Polly Klaas didn't survive her abduction.

X

Oubliette: a secret dungeon, as in certain old castles, with its only opening found in the ceiling.

Code Name: "NISEI"

CASE SUMMARY:

Mulder's near-playful investigation of an alleged alien autopsy video turns deadly serious when the video's producer is murdered and the complicity of an old Japanese plot is implicated. While investigating the man's MUFON associates, Scully struggles to understand how a band of female abductees could recognize her.

> ## EYEWITNESS STATEMENT:
>
> "The Japanese are very secretive about their espionage capabilities—and extremely careful with their intelligence data."
>
> —Frohike, Editor, Lone Gunman

DEEP BACKGROUND:

A Real Bargain at Just $29.95 (plus s&h)

It had to happen.

How long did anyone actually expect the wacky people behind *The X-Files* to resist the temptation of those notorious "Roswell autopsy videos"? Especially when their home network aired it *twice*? Waving a plate of liver in front of Eugene Tooms couldn't have been more guaranteed to get a reaction!

Run with it they did, creating the first installment of a tightly crafted two-parter that, somehow, managed to be funnier than the hokiest parts of its inspiration, yet spookier than almost anything the goriest frames of tape could suggest.

While *The X-Files* happily accepts its fictional state, the Roswell

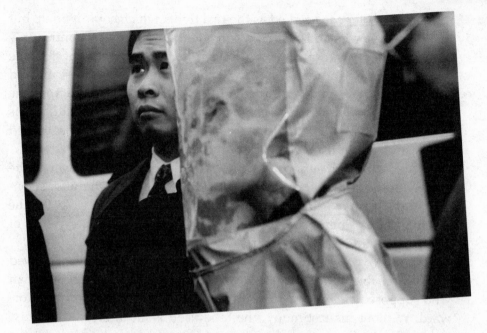

Imagine this on your resume: *X-Files* alien, non-speaking, performed under two inches of makeup and prosthetics.

TRIVIA BUSTER 10

Easy Stuff: *Take a point for each correct answer.*

1. How much did Mulder pay for his alien autopsy video?
2. What was the name of the "kitchen-table" company selling the alien autopsy videos?
3. What new "accessory" did Mulder wear in this episode?
4. What excuse does Mulder use for being in Allentown?
5. What does Mulder lose while jumping on the train?

Tougher Trivia: *These will earn you two points apiece.*

6. We saw two boxcar numbers in this episode; give one.
7. What's difficult to find in Allentown, PA, in the middle of the night?
8. What was the name of the boat in the "satellite photos"?
9. What do Scully and the women of Allentown's MUFON chapter have in common?
10. Who warned Scully to keep Mulder off the train?

"autopsy" footage is hawked as the real thing, which couldn't help but bring out believers and debunkers in equal numbers. The controversy heated up long before Fox broadcast it here, of course. The footage had already aired in half a dozen European markets; video-captured images like these circulated through UFO magazines and across the Internet. Though the footage claimed to be some fifty years old, it was just now becoming available for general "dissection" in the United States, and that in itself was part of the argument.

Why, if this film supposedly provided the definitive answer to the "alien question," was it being marketed instead of offered up for scientific study? Unlike Mulder's fictional videotape, at a mere $29.95, the commercial version of the Roswell tapes retailed for the hefty sum of thirty-five pounds sterling, nearly seventy dollars American.

The tape's present-day distributor, and its original owner, proved a tad unreliable, too. For reasons as yet unexplained, the cameraman who supposedly captured the event back in 1947 refused to come forward. Without his testimony, the tape itself is an interesting oddity, but hardly evidence. Only he can provide affidavits as to its age, the location of the filming, the name of whoever hired him, and an explanation for the convenient breaks in taping. Why, if the Defense Department hired him, didn't they keep the film? Why, if he'd seen one of the most amazing events in modern history, hadn't the cameraman himself wanted the films publicized? Even more curious, why did this startling "evidence" sit, apparently unremarked, in an attic for *fifty years*?

ANSWERS:

1. $29.95, plus shipping.
2. Rat Tail Productions.
3. An ankle holster.
4. A "video piracy thing."
5. His cellular phone.
6. 82594 or 82517.

7. A Japanese translator.
8. The *Talapus*. (You did read the sidebar, right?)
9. Little bottles and neck implants, among other things.
10. X.

YOUR SCORE _____

Could serious students of the unknown be blamed for harboring one or two suspicions of a tape that eventually came to light while its present owner searched for—get this—lost Elvis Presley footage? Ray Santilli, the British entrepreneur who set the price on the tapes, nevertheless staunchly maintains the film's authenticity and sees absolutely nothing odd in selling Disney merchandise one week and "Roswell tapes" the next.

Assuming that neither man misrepresented the contents of the tape, it certainly makes for a hell of a tale. Dragged out of his home back in the late forties, the Army photographer is hustled off to Fort Worth, Texas, into a tiny, practically featureless examination room where he's ordered to preserve the autopsy of an alien being for posterity. A secret that remained a secret for almost fifty years!

Faced with doctors decked out in heavy-duty environmental suits, did that cameraman wonder what he'd walked into? Did he demand a suit of his own? Or just stand there, calmly rolling tape as an E.B.E. was sliced open in front of him? Did he wonder about the amazing lack of uniforms in the room? And who were the civilians who never seemed to stay in frame long enough to be identified? Was he told what and whom to photograph, or are we seeing the result of his own brand of cinematography? So many questions—and no one's actually eyed the "alien" yet!

When the film finally aired, debunkers subjected every frame to the most intense scrutiny since the JFK shooting in Dallas. Were phone cords straight or curly in the 1940s? Frantic calls to unsuspecting, and previously unnoticed, telephone collectors turned up models with straight cords and others with coiled ones. Papers in the Fort Worth area found curious sleuths poring over period articles, searching out pictures of telephones, radios, and medical equipment. Local phone services and Army historians received the same treatment. One elderly doctor found himself in an unaccustomed spotlight when debunkers asked him to verify the authenticity of the procedures and equipment.

All these efforts to fail the footage on its details netted the skeptics absolutely zilch. If the film has been faked, the set dressers rival *The X-Files*, no slouches in that category, and nearly every other professional set for period authenticity.

As the focus shifted from the prosaic world of telephone collectors and retired physicians who'd rather be anonymous in Florida to the high-tech world of modern special effects, a horde of Hollywood companies now eyed the film, concentrating on the cadaver itself.

"It's good. If it's an amateur, he's missed his calling," was one special-effects technician's final comment. "It's *really* good."

So good, in fact, the body itself seems to be generating the most division between believers and skeptics. Dozens of tiny details add up to "Fake!" for some. The body fat and tissue doesn't "hang" right; it should sag toward the table instead of toward the figure's feet. Dead bodies, at least dead human bodies, don't bleed after death, certainly not enough to account for the "blood" seen welling out of one postmortem incision. Despite the "doctor's" examination of the creature's mouth, he makes absolutely no attempt to move the lips aside or open the jaw, rather normal parts of an autopsy observation. In fact, the doctor seems averse to bending, moving, or opening anything—dummies often look good until they move. As perhaps further indication that this stiff is a bit too stiff, the head *bounces* when the brain is removed to a tray!

Still, for all that, there are some items that even special-effects technicians would be delighted to bring off so well. The six-fingered hands and feet (actually a dominant genetic trait in humans) appear wonderfully proportioned. Instead of the "added-on" pinkie, each digit seems authentic. Little things, like a fine, damp membrane surrounding the brain, are the sort of details that give this "documentary" some sense of reality.

What disturbs most viewers, even fictional viewers like Mulder, is the "convenience" of the photography. Despite the "bouncing" camera lens that left viewers wishing the guy had thought to bring a tripod, some key scenes appear hopelessly contrived. Why did the camera linger on the incision that would eventually bleed if the camera operator had no preknowledge? Why didn't he just continue, as he had been doing previously, following the action of the scalpel? Why, despite his apparent ability to shoot from any angle he chose, did the photographer *never* show us more than two walls of the room? Perhaps because, like all other small, open sets, there were only two walls?

The biggest question, of course, is, *what did the Army get if all this key footage was forgotten?* Didn't they notice the gaping big holes in their film record?

In yet another of the chicken-and-egg problems so common in UFOlogy circles, believers who have no answers for the film's inconsistencies can still claim it supports the theory of alien visitations!

One of the most cherished of conspiracy theories insists that "They" developed contingency plans for any and all circumstances which might reveal the Truth. If everything has a purpose, then even the existence of a hoax must play into a larger scene. Two possibilities present themselves immediately to conspiracy fans:

1. The Desensitization Scheme. By releasing hoaxed films, the government (or shadow government, if you prefer that theory) "softens" up any public prejudices against its alien partners—without ever having to admit their existence.

2. The Discreditation Scheme. What better way to lessen the impact of any "real" film that might leak out than to deliberately create the impression that all such films are just well-done hoaxes? If, as the X-Filean Deep Throat once said, the best place to hide a lie is between two truths, then the opposite—that two lies provide an excellent hiding place for a truth—may be equally appropriate.

One last, intriguing, tie-in between the autopsy footage as aired by Fox and Fox's fictional program *The X-Files* was brought up in one of the UFO field's most accessible publications, *The Desert Rat*. According to editor Campell and his own sources, the "alien" of the autopsy, like the "aliens" found in a boxcar on reservation land, had a smallpox vaccination on its upper arm. Didn't catch that during either airing of the Alien Autopsy? Don't worry, you can always pop for the video.

eXtras:

Nisei: A common name for Japanese-Americans during the World War II era, but more accurately for the North American-born children of Japanese parents.

X

If you ever find yourself locked in a quarantine car with an "alien" and a softly glowing keypad, remember 1111471 and 101331.

X

While David Duchovny didn't actually dive from the bridge to the top of the train, he *did* race back and forth atop the moving cars to add that authentic touch to the footage. To ensure he stayed atop the boxcars, a fine cable was looped around his ankle and connected to the side of the car.

Finding a history text without this famous photo is tough.

X

 Blooper Alert! History buffs were chortling over those "satellite photos" of the *Talapus* for days after "Nisei" aired. No one expects every prop to be created from scratch, but picking as famous a picture as that taken of the *Bismarck* on May 21, 1941, cutting it into two smaller pieces, and trying to pass it off to the show's well-informed audience were . . . well, not good choices for an episode that already had X-Philes sifting through their history lessons. Real World War II aficionados recognized Grimstad Fjord (not the Panama Canal), and knew the pictures were actually taken by RAF crewmen dangling out of a Spitfire, not any combination of German, Japanese, or American optics.

Code Name: ''731''

CASE SUMMARY:

Ignoring Scully's warnings, Mulder hitches a ride aboard a train carrying an unusual passenger in its quarantine car—only to discover he's walked into a trap. Scully, picking up the threads of the investigation, quickly realizes her involvement stretches back to her own abduction—and beyond.

EYEWITNESS STATEMENT:

''The ruler of the world is no longer the country with the bravest soldiers but the greatest scientists. Unfortunately, Ishimaru began to conduct his work in secret, not sharing with those who'd risked much in giving him his asylum.''

—The Elder, Consortium Member

DEEP BACKGROUND:

UNIT 731: A Horror at Home

The X-Files' ability to hone modern horror to a fine edge and terrify its audience with the bizarre is practically unchallenged in contemporary television, but its wildest scenarios, the stuff of Sweeps Weeks, are perhaps all the more horrific in light of the *reality* that inspired them.

Mulder's brief description of Japan's Army Medical Unit 731 barely grazed the surface of the Manchurian population's agony under Dr. Ishii Shiro. He and his compatriots killed thousands with their vivisections and frost experiments, their diseases and surgical practice sessions. Yet on top of all that, like some rotten glaze, was the most inhuman and cruel abomination of all: the *American* government that would continue those experiments. While war has been used to excuse many of our cruelest acts, and would later be used to explain America's keen interest in Japanese advancements in chemical and biological techniques, the two countries couldn't have been in more different political or tactical positions.

Although it's impossible to condone any of the actions that would later make Unit 731 infamous, the original pressure to find some advantage for Japan's armed forces is easy to understand. The nation, for all its long history of warfare, is resource-poor. Unlike the United States, which in a year produced more steel in a single mill than Japan could produce in its entire country, Japan had limited tactical options. Devices of mass destruction, like those dropped on Nagasaki and Hiroshima, were still a long way from Japanese reach. There was such a debilitating shortage of raw materials for even the simplest tools of warfare that a good *can opener* was a prized possession for Japanese infantrymen. So when the Japanese Army's medical divisions, aware

TRIVIA BUSTER 11

Easy Stuff: *One point for each correct answer.*

1. What archaic disease does Scully encounter in Perkey, West Virginia?
2. "THE TRUTH IS OUT THERE" was missing from the credits for this episode. What replaced it?
3. Where was Ishimaru (aka Zama) killed?
4. The locks in the quarantine car were special. What two items were required to open a door?
5. Why can't Mulder leave car 82517 of his own volition?

Tougher Trivia: *Two well-earned points for each correct answer.*

6. What language did Mulder study in high school?
7. What code allowed the assassin into the quarantine car?
8. Mulder believed he'd seen a UFO on the docks. What did Scully believe he'd seen?
9. What was the exit code for the quarantine car?
10. Who ends up with Dr. Zama's notebook?

of the shortfalls in other areas, suggested biological and chemical methods of warfare, methods for which Japan had ample capable personnel, it seemed they'd finally found their own weapon of mass destruction.

Between the World Wars, a scientist named Ishii Shiro had been anticipating his country's future needs, and Shiro had been a busy boy. Not only did he complete a Ph.D., marry the daughter of the university president, and tour Europe's biological labs on the Army's nickel, he also made a name for himself by developing an effective water filter during a meningitis outbreak that no one has been able to prove wasn't entirely coincidental. . . .

When Japan took possession of Manchuria in 1931, Ishii Shiro was perfectly situated to head an expanding Army Medical College's bacteriological research division. And as it became clear that the ongoing war with China would provide hundreds, if not thousands, of opportunities to set *human experiments* in progress, the plans for Manchuria grew quickly.

Deciding on Harbin as a base of operations, including a sprawling facility at Pingfan in 1938, Ishii Shiro established the "Epidemic Prevention and Water Purification Department of the Kwantung Army" in August of 1932 on a virtually unlimited budget. That mouthful wouldn't become publicly known as Unit 731 until 1941, when its sister operation, the "Department of Veterinary Disease Prevention of the Kwantung Army," was generally acknowledged as the almost equally infamous Unit 100. As a full colonel, with some 3,000 Japanese citizens

ANSWERS:

1. Hansen's disease, aka leprosy.
2. APOLOGY IS POLICY.
3. A bathroom aboard the train.
4. A key card and a code number.
5. There's a bomb on board.
6. French.
7. 1111471.
8. The remains of a Russian submarine.
9. 101331.
10. The Cigarette-Smoking Man and a Japanese translator.

YOUR SCORE _____

Would Scully really have mistaken these guys for victims of Leprosy if she'd gotten a good look at them?

working under him, and with an unlimited pool of Chinese laborers and "subjects," Ishii Shiro played God to his heart's content, and trained hundreds of doctors in his own school of medicine.

One of those doctors, Yuasa Ken, freely discusses their activities. "I asked the doctor who was about to administer lumbar anesthesia if he wasn't going to disinfect the point of injection. 'What are you talking about? We're going to kill him,' he replied." It wasn't long before they stopped bothering with the anesthesia altogether. . . . Scores of Manchurians, sprayed with water, found themselves begging for a different sort of numbness as they stumbled naked around the compound in the freezing night air. Most didn't survive until morning. Those who did often found themselves flayed alive as 731 scientists "collected representative skin samples" of those who proved cold-resistant.

Yuasa Ken's rationalization for sacrificing hundreds of human beings? ". . . there weren't enough surgeons available. Even ophthalmologists or pediatricians had to be able to do it . . . so they practiced. . . . It was easier to get men to fight if they thought there was a doctor to treat them when they were hit." Clearly, Yuasa Ken and his fellow doctors never considered the possibility of carrying out their practice sessions on their fellow Japanese.

With medics chosen for their ability to carry rifles, and Japanese Red Cross nurses helping dismember civilians, callous handling of the dead and dying shouldn't be a shock. . . . "It gave us pause to think of throwing him, still breathing, into the hole out back, so the director injected air into his heart with a syringe. Another doctor—he's alive today—and I then had to try to strangle him with string. Still he wouldn't die. Finally, an old noncom said, 'Honorable Doctor, he'll die if you give him a shot of anesthesia.' Afterward we threw him into the hole."

It's no small measure of 731's terrorism that its members, in part, aggravated the civilian population's own insensitivity to horror—if only through unending grief. From individual murder to mass extermination, Unit 731 was nothing if not flexible. As if history hadn't already proved the point, Unit 731 released hundreds of plague-infested rats to see if they could spread death as effectively as high-altitude bombs. They did. In a village of forty-two families, forty-three people died. The rest, to survive, scattered, desperate to halt the spread of disease. One man recalls, "I remember the scene of my sister's death as if it were yesterday. She was left in a small hut by herself. No one looked after her. When I found out she was dead, I went to look. Her neck was swollen, and she died with her eyes wide open." Cholera, anthrax, and a host of other diseases were introduced into water supplies and food stores. In one case, cholera-laced candies were distributed to children at a local festival.

Fifty years later, victims of Unit 731—who included Koreans, Manchurians, Mongolians, Russians, and captured American POWs—are still awaiting an apology for their misery, an acknowledgment of their plight, and justice. While the Nuremberg trials were meting out sentences to German war criminals, the "Asian incident" was being studiously ignored. Just as Operation Paper Clip had attempted to secure German war secrets against the threat of a Japanese assault, so did the Americans quickly make deals with the men and women of Unit 731 against the threat of an escalating Cold War.

For some time, various sources claimed they'd been unaware of the atrocities, but closer examination rapidly dispels any such excuse. In

1949, in the Soviet Union, the only Japanese scientists ever to be tried for war crimes stood trial in Khabarovsk, and the results of those investigations were made public in the widely distributed "The Trial of Former Servicemen of the Japanese Army Charged with Manufacturing and Employing Bacteriological Weapons" (Foreign Language Publishing House, Moscow, 1950).

Even before those officers were found, however, China had asked for international help on no less than *thirty-seven* different occasions, citing mass exterminations due to biological and chemical agents as well as the slaughter of both civilians and POWs in the "medical facilities."

The August 1942 issue of the *Rocky Mountain Medical Journal* presented an article entitled "Japanese Use the Chinese as 'Guinea Pigs' to Test Germ Warfare."

In 1942, the United States itself protested Japan's use of bacterial bombs over Changde. Of course, it was the same president, Roosevelt, who just weeks before had authorized American facilities to begin their own biological warfare research. Small wonder the government didn't continue its protests too loudly.

Claims of ignorance are no more supportable now than they were fifty years ago. While dozens of Germans were sent to their deaths or imprisoned, not a single Japanese scientist was imprisoned after 1960 or handed a death penalty. In fact, under agreements with the United States, no records of American investigations were ever published. Ishii Shiro, like most of the 731 doctors, returned to a thriving civilian practice and a prominent position at an important university. To claim, as *The X-Files* did, that these scientists were given free access to the United States, its universities, and its laboratories is easy—and completely true. Fearful of disclosures at home, many 731 doctors immigrated to the United States and, without a word about their "internships," were accepted into hospitals and teaching positions.

Given their complete freedom of movement, and the United States' predilection for collecting foreign science and scientists, it's hardly surprising that *The X-Files* could incorporate 731's history into an American-based plotline so easily. It's all too likely that some form of those experiments continued within American borders. As early as the Korean conflict, both the Chinese and the Korean governments claimed *American* forces were employing biological agents. As recently as the Gulf War, American soldiers were inoculated against disease strains that supposedly died out in the labs when the United States supposedly stopped their own biological-warfare experiments. And, in between those, the United States was happily injecting its own citizens with radioactive plutonium. . . .

Like Japan, the United States was also a little late in signing the Geneva protocol banning chemical and bacteriological warfare. It took America fifty years to sign on the dotted line.

> "It is scary. It's outrageous to murder a person. Yet it's far worse to forget that you've done it. That's the most horrible thing imaginable!"
>
> —Yuasa Ken

In 1995, we might be hard pressed to decide who was doing the forgetting.

By combining historical facts with the Roswell crash, *The X-Files* brought together two events, supposedly contemporary in terms of time, and gave us the answer to the "What if?" we might have been asking if the work of Unit 731—and American involvement—had been publicized at the time.

eXtras:

For those with slo-mo on their VCR and a working knowledge of Japanese, the doctor's journal contained some interesting stuff. . . . six months . . . final solution . . . space alien . . . and . . . secret experiments . . .

X-REFERENCE:

Yet Another Alphabet Organization?

With the FBI and the CIA already implicated in their ongoing plots and machinations, it was just a matter of time before *The X-Files* got around to the "other" organization in the intelligence community triangle, the National Security Agency. Maybe its out-in-the-boonies address was what let them go unnoticed for so long. Unlike the CIA and the FBI, headquartered in Washington, the NSA settled into an average community over in equally average Maryland. But it's more than the view that separates this organization from the others.

Hoover's politics might have been unfathomable at times, but he understood that one of the best weapons he could give his agents was a "reputation." Public relations was, and remains, an important part of the FBI's operating procedure. While it was sound business to keep technical and forensic advances under the Bureau's hat until they were needed, the news of each and every capture was released to the press in carefully orchestrated stages. The CIA followed a similar program. The NSA tallied its greatest triumphs when *no one* realized how successful it had been.

That's the way it works when your job is protecting the nation's communications while infiltrating foreign intelligence information. The NSA, and the affiliated Central Security Service, aren't point operatives. Instead, they provide some of the most specialized technicians and security equipment to dozens of other government, and occasionally civilian, agencies. Established under the authority of the Secretary of Defense, it's the only one of the three to be officially affiliated with the Department of Defense, the only one that exercises any control over the intelligence departments of all branches of military service. Where the FBI and the CIA must walk carefully, the NSA is a routine observer.

The NSA's basic purpose is twofold. First, to provide whatever personnel and equipment are required to ensure the security of both classified and unclassified information. Second, to monitor, organize, and collect foreign signals. Both aims are undertaken in order to provide American agencies with current, secure intelligence. It's hardly surprising that a considerable portion of the NSA's resources is devoted to cryptology in all its forms—or that NSA personnel work closely with the intelligence sections within the DoD, the Department of Justice (DoJ) including the FBI, the Treasury, Energy, and State departments, and the CIA.

Of all the agencies *The X-Files'* garrote-toting assassin could have claimed as his own, the NSA is perhaps the most unlikely. Few of its agents could be called your average field operatives; most of them are code makers and breakers, technicians who track data like the K-9 Corps traces drugs, linguists, translators, and communications/data processing specialists. The agents who contributed to the first mainframe computers, the first solid-state computer, the development of the tape cassette, and semiconductor technology don't appear to be the type to kill elderly scientists in bathrooms, and the assassin himself seemed remarkably lacking in any other obvious abilities.

The NSA's operatives are also the least likely to be stumped by current technology. Ongoing professional development became so important within the NSA/CSS that a separate section, the National Cryptologic School, was established to deal with the escalating demand for upgrading. It's an indication of the school's standards that many sections of the Department of Defense send their personnel to the NSA training programs by choice. That tight relationship with the armed forces also separates the NSA from its intelligence "cousins" in Washington; the NSA is the only agency with both civilian and military personnel in the ranks.

Perhaps being outside the Washington League affects attitude as well, for the NSA often seems as much a community as any town.

- The NSA is the single largest employer in Anne Arundel County and one of the largest in the State of Maryland.
- The NSA has its own Environmental Management Services division, and the NSA is one of only a handful of federal agencies that voluntarily exceeds all federal, state, and local environmental regulations.
- The NSA's Recycling Program collected over 250 tons of newspaper, general paper, aluminum, and cardboard last year.
- The NSA has been an exceptional member of the Association for Commuter Transportation (ACT), a national organization of transportation professionals in the public and private sectors.
- The NSA has sponsored a blood donor program for twenty-four years. Over 200 agency members roll up their sleeves on a regular basis, donating in excess of 1,900 units.
- The National Security Agency not only helps sponsor bone marrow screenings biannually, its *members* have nearly 1,900 registered bone marrow volunteers, several of whom are delighted to have become active donors already.
- Aware of the distance between emerging technologies and interfaces to make those technologies available to persons with disabilities, the NSA opened the Center for Computer Assistive Technology to help close that gap.
- The NSA has been recognized by the State of Maryland for its employees' generous contributions of thousands of volunteer hours to Maryland schools each year—teaching, coaching, and assisting in various ways.

Hardly the place to hide an agent with a fondness for piano wire.

Maybe that sense of pride and community was the driving force behind the NSA's recent unveiling of the National Cryptologic Museum. Here, after years of waiting for its contributions to be declassified, the National Security Agency finally gets its chance to shine. In a succinct history of cryptology, the museum's exhibits include equipment, personnel biographies, and samples of the codes that stumped Americans and their enemies.

One of the exhibits is an absolute must for X-Philes who enjoyed the notion of The Cigarette-Smoking Man being defeated by a band of Navajo with great memories. The Code Talkers' contribution to the

NSA

Want the romance of a career in the intelligence community without the inconvenience of Kevlar vests and whizzing bullets? Find yourself cast more in the mold of The Lone Gunmen than the dashing agents Mulder and Scully? Then the NSA may be the spot for you.

Not only does the NSA regularly fill positions in a number of fields, it even sponsors *summer and student* positions. An impressive item for any résumé. Permanent, full-time positions include the broad categories of mathematics, computer and electrical/electronics engineering, computer science, and a number of language studies (Asian, Middle Eastern, and Slavic, with the exception of Russian). Clerical, computer, analytic, and accounting positions are filled in every category of employment from permanent, full-time, to the after-school positions filled through the NSA's High School Work Study Program.

FULL-TIME POSITIONS: In addition to the support and clerical staff hired each year, specialists are always needed.

Mathematicians: Mathematicians of every stripe are employed by the NSA in cryptography, cryptanalysis, engineering, data traffic analysis, and computer security.

Computer and Electrical/Electronics Engineers: Engineers tackle the design, development, testing, and evaluation of electronic communication and signal processing systems; pattern recognition; signals analysis; and the design of special-purpose computers, antennas, and radar systems. Engineers also address complex issues associated with providing security for our critical national information systems and networks. The complex issues include the potential loss or corruption of information due to network penetration. These multidisciplinary assignments will reach to such rapidly advancing areas as optics, lasers, acoustics, and microprocessors.

Computer Scientists: The NSA's computer scientists work in one of the world's largest and most advanced computer and data processing centers in positions addressing such varied fields as data base management and artificial intelligence.

Language Specialists: Language specialists at the NSA work on translation, transcription, documentation, and analysis projects, which allow them to hone their language skills daily while working on real-world problems.

COLLEGE-LEVEL EMPLOYMENT OPPORTUNITIES: Not only does the NSA recruit from the best professionals the nation has to offer, it also assists promising college students through a number of "earn and learn" programs.

Cooperative Education (Co-op) Program: The Co-op program invites students to bring their "book knowledge" to real-world problems during a series of increasingly challenging work terms. The variety of fields open to students provides a distinct advantage to those who've yet to determine exactly which area will be their chosen career path.

Summer Program: For college students who aren't in a Cooperative program, but could still benefit from the challenging environment of the NSA, there's the Summer Program, which hires those who've completed their junior year for full-time summer positions.

Director's Summer Program: The Director's Summer Program is a twelve-week summer workshop program for outstanding college mathematics students. Participants work with NSA mathematicians on exciting cryptomathematical problems. The program is highly competitive and intended primarily for students between their junior and senior years, but exceptional freshmen, sophomores, and graduate students will be considered.

The Undergraduate Training Program: The Undergraduate Training Program presents a unique opportunity for a select few of the nation's finest high school students. The UTP is available for students, particularly minorities, who will attend college full-time and major in computer science, electrical or computer engineering, mathematics, or various foreign languages (depending on the NSA's language requirements). Students receive college tuition and a year-round salary, work every summer, and have a guaranteed job with the NSA after graduation. Participants are required to work for the NSA after college graduation for at least one and a half times their length of study. This program is highly competitive.

HIGH-SCHOOL-LEVEL PROGRAMS: The NSA sponsors two opportunities for high school students.

High School Work Study Program: High school students can find part-time employment within the NSA, working for sixteen to twenty-five hours per week during their senior year and receiving many of the benefits of their college- and professional-level co-workers. The program is designed to provide participants with practical experience in clerical, computer, analytic, and accounting fields.

Gifted and Talented Program: This is a summer program (thirty-two hours per week) allowing exceptional juniors and seniors the opportunity to work with the NSA's best in the math, computer science, and engineering fields. The students' mentors have accepted the responsibility of assisting them in developing their technical competency to its highest level.

As with most government positions, benefits are generous and extend to all programs, including those of part-time and high school employees. Salaries are equal to, if not higher than, their private-sector equivalents. In many of the college-level positions, tuition, travel benefits, and continued professional development are all part of the package. Not to mention the nifty badge.

First World War is chronicled in considerable detail, including the involvement of the Choctaw, Comanche, Kiowa, Winnebago, Hopi, Cherokee, Seminoles, and Navajo. The refinements made by the Army before 1941, and the Navajo-only version that proved so completely trustworthy, are also displayed.

If the image of an organization that could include both *The X-Files'* Albert Hosteen and its sly assassin seems a tad surreal, that's hardly surprising. Unless the NSA is even better at keeping secrets than anyone knows, it is also the agency with the lowest number of agent-involved incidents.

Code Name: "REVELATIONS"

CASE SUMMARY:

When Scully suggests a Divine origin for the stigmatic-type wounds of a young boy from Ohio, it's Mulder's turn to play skeptic, but there's one thing they agree on. The boy has made the short list of a serial killer with religious convictions outside the norm.

EYEWITNESS STATEMENT:

"Either we're dealing with a psychotic religious fanatic who's hell-bent on exposing these kind of frauds, or [with] a less problematic psycho who harbors a murderous resentment toward the church, or maybe it's just a *very* disgruntled altar boy."

—Special Agent Fox Mulder

DEEP BACKGROUND:

Between Fact and Faith

When the ill-fated character Reverend Findley declared, ". . . miracles are wonders by nature, they need no rationale, no justification," he was preaching to the converted. For most, such complete faith, whether in science or in higher sentience, comes less easily. Confronted by something as inexplicable as the stigmata, or the greater question of sainthood, our innate curiosity kicks in, asking, "Why? How?"

Had marks like the stigmata existed solely in religious histories or been as completely unquantifiable as prayer, they'd likely have remained strictly a spiritual issue. In fact, the original secular investigations of the phenomenon actually had nothing to do with the stigmata themselves, concentrating instead on a series of incidents afflicting victims of personality disorders.

During a hypnotic past-life regression, Ann Dowling returned to her waking self with distinct bruises consistent with the violent death of her "previous self" Sarah Williams. *The Lancet*, Britain's most prestigious medical journal, reported the case of an Army officer who, after dreaming he'd been tied up, awoke with welts deep enough to draw blood around both his arms. The suggestion of self-mutilation in these and other cases quickly fell by the wayside under experimental conditions that would satisfy *both* Mulder's and Scully's expectations.

Another widely publicized case involved a famous victim of multiple personality syndrome. While in a normal mental state, Chris Sizemore ("Eve" of *The Three Faces of Eve*) remembered a traumatic childhood event. Mentally transported back to her much younger self, she recalled the day she'd caught her dress afire and received scars still visible nearly forty years later. The adult Chris rolled across the floor, attempting to douse the unseen flames, screaming for her mother, totally unaware of her present surroundings. Horrified, her family found that the skin around the original burn had turned nearly purple. The old scars were puckered and inflamed. The cold cloths they applied to the "injury" steamed.

These people's very real anguish was unmistakable, but the only connection appeared to be their occasional dissociation from "normal" mental states. No doubt based in part on the involvement of "Eve," investigators began reviewing others with multiple-personality disorders. Few subjects proved as spectacular as Chris, but dozens exhibited similar physiological oddities. Clair Beauville displayed chronic psoriasis, but less than an hour after emerging, her alter ego Candy Belle sported a flawless rosy complexion. Robert Connery's allergy to dogs was well documented, yet any one of his thirteen subpersonas could have worked for the local vet.

With the broad parameters of the phenomenon well described, no researcher worth his or her salt could ignore the long history of stigmatization. Whatever their origin, the marks of the stigmata were evidently an "unexplained physiological phenomenon." That prayer and meditation qualified as "altered states of consciousness" was already well established, easily proven under lab conditions. Add in the stig-matic's frequent tendency to "speak in other voices," suffer amnesia during and after a religious experience, and refer to himself in the third person, and the similarities between the experiences of the stig-matic and the multiple personality are even more evident.

Even so, the sensitive nature of stigmatization's place in several major religions might have kept it out of the scientific arena even longer if not for a coincidence that put a woman suffering from multi-ple personalities in the home of her physician, Dr. Lechler, over Easter. The woman, called Anna for anonymity, had, in addition to the usual symptoms of multiple personality syndrome (MPS), a predilection toward hypochondria. Whenever faced with stressful situations, any-thing from visiting her family to deciding on a course of treatment, Anna developed symptoms of some illness, on one occasion actually coughing up blood as if she'd contracted TB! After Anna attended an Easter lecture on the Crucifixion, Dr. Lechler was understandably worried.

That concern was well placed.

Within hours, Anna complained of pain in her hands and feet.

TRIVIA BUSTER 12

Easy Stuff: *Take a single point for each correct answer.*

1. What was unusual about Reverend Findley's "vestry"?
2. How did Mulder describe Owen Jarvis, Kevin's kidnapper?
3. What did Scully find among the burns on Owen's neck?
4. What elusive scent did Scully claim came from Owen Jarvis's corpse?
5. What did Simon Gates do to the doorknob of Kevin Kreider's house?

Tougher Trivia: *These are worth their two-point rewards.*

6. Where did Reverend Findley preach?
7. What odd syndrome did Mulder believe Gates suffered from?
8. How did Simon Gates get into the motel bathroom?
9. Where were Kevin's wounds?
10. Where does Mr. Kreider's cryptic "full circle" comment lead Scully?

As Anna had already agreed to and submitted to many sessions of hypnotherapy to diagnose and treat her illness, Lechler decided to try something different to gauge the depth of his patient's suggestibility. Instead of hypnotically suggesting Anna's "illness" fade, he instructed her to continue thinking of the lecture and of a figure already familiar to her—St. Francis, perhaps the most famous of the stigmatics. On seeing her again in the morning, he immediately put his patient under, ordering her to cast all such thoughts from her mind. Visible on the tops and bottoms of both hands and feet were open lesions.

Perhaps suffering a twinge of guilt, Lechler sat down with Anna,

ANSWERS:

1. Its makeup table and lights.
2. Homer Simpson's evil twin.
3. Fingerprints.
4. The smell of flowers.
5. He melted it with his touch.
6. The First Church of Redemption in Waynesburg, PA.
7. Jerusalem Syndrome.
8. He bent the bars outside the window.
9. On his hands and side.
10. To Simon Gates's recycling facility, the 21st Century Recycling Plant.

YOUR SCORE _____

explaining the difficulty of placing stigmatization into the investigative side of science and detailing what he believed was at work in the shadowy areas of her mind.

Anna suffered from MPS, hypochondria, and bouts of depression, but she evidently was a strong woman despite those many obstacles. Not only did she shrug off the questionable curve tossed into her treatment the previous night, she encouraged Lechler to take whatever steps were necessary to pin down these mysterious happenings in a more traditionally controlled setting.

In the course of the next several months, on cue from Lechler, Anna's hands and feet bled repeatedly, bloody tears rained down her cheeks, welts from a suggested "crown of thorns" rose around her head, and her shoulders ached from dragging her imaginary cross. Considering that, regardless of their psychosomatic origins, these "injuries" caused real pain, Anna's desire to understand her condition must easily have matched Lechler's. If nothing else, her cooperation forever ended any hint that she engaged in self-mutilation.

Experimentation over a ten-year period, involving scores of volunteers, demonstrated beyond a doubt that stigmatization was an authentic occurrence. Unlike *The X-Files'* Reverend Findley, with his IV bags and tubing, none of the stigmatics studied ever objected to observation and none evidenced any desire to fake symptoms or seek the spotlight. Quite the contrary.

Perhaps reflecting the vast majority of scientists' adherence to a religious affiliation, these investigations in no way undermined Lechler's own Catholic beliefs—or those of Anna.

While stigmata are clearly linked to other syndromes, the *mechanism* capable of opening spontaneous wounds and healing them in fractions of the time normally required has yet to be fully understood. "Physician, heal thyself" takes on a rather different meaning in light of these results.

Of the many indicators of sainthood, "mind over matter" can account for only a few scattered incidents. The "incorruptible" nature of saints, the floral odor attributed to their remains, the healing obtained at sites associated with them, and other signs of favor can't be ascribed to the frailties of a human mind long since dead. If we're all so susceptible to suggestion as to continue the incidents through our own suggestibility, then perhaps the "reality" of a miracle is, after all, inconsequential and faith really is a force in its own right.

eXtras:

St. Ignatius A diligent search for a biblical reference to St. Ignatius will likely be fruitless. Of the two modern-day saints of that name, one found religion after being hit by a cannonball and the other followed Peter as head of the Roman Catholic Church. Neither is credited with the ability to be in two places at once.

Guardian Angels *The X-Files* may be solely responsible for a revival of Owen as a popular name. To date, two X-Filean guardian angels have had it as part of their name. Owen was to watch over Kevin; Nurse Owens did an admirable job of caring for her charge, Scully.

X

Of the 330 individuals who've been reported as stigmatics, sixty— who've also exhibited other mystical happenings—have been either canonized or beatified by the Roman Catholic Church.

X

 Blooper Alert! The thermometer popped so casually into Kevin Kreider's mouth sported the brilliant red end marking it as a *rectal* thermometer, something neither the school nurse nor *Dr.* Scully seemed to notice.

Code Name:
"WAR OF THE COPROPHAGES"

CASE SUMMARY:

Escaping the misery of an apartment fumigation, Mulder heads for his old stomping grounds on the Vineyard. Scully's off-hours, however, are repeatedly interrupted by her partner's investigation of "killer roaches." As the deaths add up, though, even Scully begins to suspect that something smells bad on the island.

EYEWITNESS STATEMENT:

"Scully, if an alien civilization were technologically advanced enough to build and send artificially intelligent probes to the farthest reaches of space, might they not have also been able to perfect the extraction of methane fuel from manure, an abundant and replenishing energy source on a planet filled with dung-producing creatures?"

—Special Agent Fox Mulder

DEEP BACKGROUND:

There's Just Nothing Like a Little Mass Hysteria

There's just nothing like a little mass hysteria to bring a community together. Whether its individuals then decide to dance in the streets, scratch imaginary lesions, or massacre innocent little cockroaches as the citizens of Miller's Grove did doesn't seem to matter as long as they do it *en masse*.

People have been getting together to do the inexplicable for centuries. One of the earliest "objectively" reported incidents began in thirteenth-century Italy in the tiny village of Thepilia. Thinking they'd been bitten by hordes of roaming tarantulas, the citizens threw themselves into the streets, screaming, shaking violently, and, in dozens of cases, *dancing*. One in ten victims fell into convulsions. Scarcely anyone escaped some symptom. Yet, oddly enough, no one ever produced a spider. . . .

Thepilia's population, no more than a thousand at any time, nevertheless still traveled, traded, came in contact with other people; and before long, the "condition" had spread to neighboring communities! In areas where no tarantulas had ever been spotted, *tarantism* became known as St. Vitus's dance. The raving, the jumping, the convulsions— and, of course, the dancing!—continued unabated. By the end of the century, not a single European country was spared an outbreak of St. Vitus's dance, but its association with tarantulas was nearly forgotten.

India, in 1634, provided a particularly spectacular example of mass madness. The brutal slaughter of an elderly grandmother, Idhiri Anwarahadrani, by a band of young men had already put the community under considerable stress. The location of the murder, inside a local temple, likely added another layer of horror to the event. When Idhiri's grandson fainted at her funeral, remained unconscious for three days, and awoke claiming to have had a vision of his grandmother taking vengeance on the town, which had yet to punish the murdering sons of a high-caste family, the entire population was primed for, at the very least, one hellish mass anxiety attack.

First friends of the Anwarahadrani family, then their servants, then neighbors, and eventually most of the village claimed to hear Idhiri's final wails for help just before they were all struck blind. Even perfectly healthy adults from outside the community fell victim after entering the temple. It's probably not surprising that the youths involved in the murder turned up dead, or that the affliction cursing the town disappeared after their bodies were found.

To get a grip on the mechanisms that science *thinks* fuel group delusions, start with individual susceptibility. Though it's easy to suggest that certain groups, like the "mentally infirm," "uneducated," or plain "gullible," could be swayed by an exaggerated case of peer pressure, that doesn't begin to explain how entire communities, a broad spectrum of personality types, could be affected so uniformly.

A study completed in 1992, however, suggests rather convincingly that almost anyone can be persuaded to go counter to his or her usual beliefs without any form of "brainwashing" in the traditional sense (i.e. chemicals, sensory deprivation, or physical abuse).

In the experimental setup, which supposedly tested the effectiveness of several analgesics, fourteen subjects were gathered together in a single room and given buttons they believed would deliver an electrical current to fourteen other volunteers across the room from them. In reality, the buttons were dummies and the fourteen "volunteers" on the "hot" end of the setup were actors from local drama groups. From time to time, four "doctors" wandered back and forth between the actors, ostensibly checking their condition, reassuring the subjects that all was well. On the advice of these "doctors," the subjects were eventually convinced to administer electrical doses far exceeding the limits they'd been told were safe—despite one actor's convincing portrayal of a woman in heart failure!

TRIVIA BUSTER 13

Easy Stuff: *Take a single point for each of these no-brainers.*

1. What company did the exterminator work for?
2. Why was Mulder in Massachusetts?
3. What movie do characters in this episode keep referring to?
4. What shampoo does Scully favor for her dog?
5. What was unusual about the exoskeleton Mulder found?

Tougher Trivia: *These will earn you your two points.*

6. What does Scully suggest as a cause of death for the doctor found in the bathroom?
7. What was Dr. Berenbaum's first name?
8. What were the boys burning in their homemade "lab"?
9. Other than being "hung like a club-tailed dragonfly," what was odd about the sample bug Mulder provided?
10. What was the motto of Dr. Eckerle's company, Alt-Fuels Inc.?

Only one volunteer, out of a field of seven doctors, two nurses, two firefighters, and three clergymen, refused to complete the tests.

In an after-the-fact investigation of the subjects' reasons for inflicting what appeared to be considerable misery on their fellow humans, a number of consistent responses arose. First, the subjects' faith in the professional acumen of the attending "physicians" was absolute. Second, all subjects believed they were acting for a "greater good," which was reinforced by their co-experimenters' careers in service to their communities. Third, the subjects felt they were under intense pressure to resolve the problem given them. Fourth, perhaps most important, none of the *volunteers* made an overt attempt to escape their own misery, which confirmed the subjects' growing, if warped, belief in the urgency of the experiment. It seems even the most reasonable people will put aside their convictions if a "community" interest is at stake.

And that community interest isn't always obvious.

Sixteen students and five of their teachers came down with completely inexplicable symptoms, which even included elevated levels of carboxyhemoglobin, two weeks after the start of the Persian Gulf War. The symptoms disappeared when the school decided to wait until after the conflict before including it in their Current Affairs courses.

With so many incidents of mass hysteria including elements of apparent hypochondria, current psychological investigators are beginning to wonder if rises in the incidence of "universal allergies" and chronic fatigue syndrome are, in part, responses to fast-paced modern life and fears about the future.

ANSWERS:

1. Dr. Bugger Exterminator.
2. To investigate some lights in the sky while escaping the fumigation of his own apartment.
3. *Planet of the Apes*.
4. Die, Flea, Die!
5. It appeared to be metal.
6. Brain aneurism due to excessive "strain."
7. Bambi.
8. Manure, to obtain methane fumes.
9. It was mechanical.
10. "Waste Is a Terrible Thing to Waste."

YOUR SCORE _____

The most famous of the modern cases occurred in quiet Berry, Alabama. The area's kids, about four hundred of them, attend—what else?—Berry Elementary School, the most average of schools, and until 1973 did nothing the least bit out of the ordinary.

On May 11, however, all that changed as three teachers and seventy students, twenty of them unconscious, arrived at Fayette County Hospital. In between bouts of fainting and throwing up, the children scratched and screamed. Before the end of the day, more frightening symptoms, including numbness and paralysis, turned up. By the time the first terrified parents arrived, some of the children were bleeding freely from a multitude of scratches. With no cause apparent, local authorities searched everywhere, trying to confirm or deny possibilities that ranged from toxic contagions to a mysterious new form of Legionnaires' disease to insect swarms to radiation.

When the children's conditions appeared to stabilize, and no new symptoms developed, dozens of investigators began interviewing them. Eventually a bizarre little story came to light—all beginning with a single little girl who couldn't sit still.

According to the amalgamated reports, the fifth-grader arrived back at school after recovering from a skin rash. The remaining tickle, however, soon had her scratching, which turned the tickle to a burn, which made her scratch more, which . . . Well, eventually her contortions so disturbed the class that she was asked to sit in the hall. During the morning recess her friends crowded around, and before long, they were scratching madly. Attempts to wash off whatever was making them itch didn't work and several began to panic. Other children in the bathroom gathered around to see what was causing the fuss, and by lunchtime, kids were scratching violently in every single classroom. Trying to relieve the itching with alcohol only irritated the already raw skin, and almost before anyone realized what was happening, the school had dozens of screaming children to deal with. Gradually, the authorities began to suspect they were dealing with mass hysteria.

Bit by bit, medical sleuths ruled out cause after cause for the "epidemic." The outbreak had begun before lunch—ruling out a toxic substance in the food; water was out because not all the children with symptoms had used school fountains or tried to wash in the bathrooms. Except for a few students with slightly elevated temperatures, no fever was present, and blood studies showed absolutely nothing abnormal—making the idea of a bacterial or viral infection highly unlikely. The rapid recovery of several students eventually convinced investigators that this wasn't biological in origin.

Which left?

Allergies? Aside from the fact that seventy children and a few adults suddenly developing the same allergy at the same time would in itself be a medical miracle, the scratching patterns indicated specific patches of itchiness, unlikely in an allergic reaction to noncontact allergens.

Toxic substances? Air, water, soil, dust, fabric, flooring, everything that could possibly trap a toxin was collected, shipped out, and analyzed. Nothing.

The Berry case is still an open investigation, but no one expects to find a single causative factor, not even a tarantula or a cockroach.

Cockroaches are more likely to be found in Dr. Bambi's pseudo-kitchen than in the variou blobs of manure featured in "War of the Coprophages."

THE AMAZING COCKROACH

The cockroach may not be an alien probe, but it is definitely bizarre.

- Cockroaches can live a week without a head. It dies only because, without a mouth, it can't drink water.
- How does a cockroach show its displeasure? Like a human. It has salivary glands and spits when it's disturbed. Oh, yes, and as Dr. Bambi told us, it takes a bath if handled by a human.
- Cockroaches have eighteen knees.
- The world's largest roach, a native of South America, is six inches long with a one-foot wingspan.
- Want to confuse a cockroach? Shine a red light on it; it can't see in red light.
- A roach can hold its breath for forty minutes.
- The average American cockroach can run three miles in an hour.
- Ever see a white cockroach like the one in the last scene of "War of the Coprophages"? It's just shed its skin.
- The H.M.S. *Bounty* was a deluxe roach motel. Bligh had to disinfect it with boiling water.
- Cockroaches used to be considered lucky in Europe and a common gift at housewarming parties.
- As Scully said, some people develop allergies to cockroaches. While anaphylactic shock is a possibility, more common symptoms are skin rashes and respiratory congestion.
- The cockroach's heart is just a tube with valves for pumping blood backward and forward. Heart failure isn't going to be found on any roach-y death certificates, though—the heart can stop beating for months without harming the cockroach.

eXtras:

"What Is . . . *Breakfast at Tiffany's*" Did you notice what Scully was reading in this episode? It was *Breakfast at Tiffany's*, a title David Duchovny is unlikely to forget anytime soon. His first appearance in a Celebrity *Jeopardy* match, against opponents Stephen King and Lynn Redgrave, began incredibly well for him. He led throughout, showing a range of knowledge somewhat rare among actors, whose busy careers often leave them little time for anything else. When it came time for Final *Jeopardy*, and the category appeared tailor-made for the former English Lit. major, it began to look like a runaway. What English major—what English major *from New York*—couldn't take "Capote" and "famous hotel restaurant" and come up with *Breakfast at Tiffany's*? Well, David Duchovny for one. Small wonder his set mates rub it in once in a while.

X

Dr. Bugger's representative blew the geological-era section of the training manual. Cockroaches are about 280 million years old, which puts them in the carboniferous era.

X

One of the best-known of the mass hysteria stories is Orson Welles's classic radio play *War of the Worlds*. "War of the Coprophages" paid tribute to it by setting the events in Miller's Grove. Welles's tale was played out in Grover's Mill . . . just down the road from each other?

X

Residents of the Vancouver area probably giggled when they saw "G.F. Strong" stenciled on the back of the wheelchair, G.F. Strong being a rehab center in Vancouver.

X

After seeing Die, Flea, Die! dog shampoo, and the Die, Bug, Die! insect spray, you've just got to wonder if Darin Morgan was a fan of that horrid horror flick *Die, Monster, Die!*

X

 Blooper Alert! Thomas Crapper didn't exactly "invent" the flush toilet. The Romans had flush toilets several thousand years ago. What he did do, very well, was make it possible for all of us to head off to bed and *not* have to listen to the water running all night. He invented the thingie that closes off the water supply after the flush. If you actually want the whole story, try *Flushed with Pride: The Story of Thomas Crapper* by Wallace Reyburn.

Code Name: "SYZYGY"

CASE SUMMARY:

Instead of horned beasts, pentagrams, and midnight masses—the stuff of which a satanic cult investigation should be made—Mulder and Scully are confounded by a haunting perfume, malfunctioning TVs, killer garage springs, and two teenage girls best described as . . . cosmic.

EYEWITNESS STATEMENT:

"I don't suppose there have been any actual reports of stolen infants? Or of mass graves being uncovered anywhere in town? Or that you found an altar or any other evidence of a black mass?"

—Special Agent Dana Scully

DEEP BACKGROUND:

When All Else Fails: Satanic Ritual Abuse

The McMartin trial, which linked satanic rituals, day-care centers, and child abuse in the American mind for all of its *seven* years, obviously had an impact on Carter and his team of writers. Not only was it prominently mentioned during the "Syzygy" episode as an example of the "witch-hunt" mentality, it also contributed the "naked movie-star games" line, a direct quote from testimony given during the trial.

McMartin also spawned an unusual form of "copycat" crime. Instead of criminals jumping on the modus operandi of other supposed criminals, whole communities, prosecutors, and law enforcement personnel jumped on the *crime* itself. Satanic ritual abuse, practically unheard-of before the McMartin case, became a "syndrome" in about the same amount of time it took the media to latch onto the outlandish crime and pop psychologists to work up a list of signs and symptoms indicative of this latest evil.

If nothing else, the publicity surrounding McMartin and other "satanic ritual" trials provided the impetus for a full-scale investigation of ritual slayings, and illustrated important lessons for those trying to prosecute legitimate child (or even animal) abuse cases. Even if not quite the ". . . wild beast entering in on a black mass, the drinking of blood, the sacrifice of an infant . . . or a blond virgin . . ." that Scully predicted in the De Boom case, there are common factors among these mass paranoia cases, items that were worked almost seamlessly into the darkly humorous "Syzygy."

Almost inevitably, the accused is closely connected with the youngest members of the community. In "Syzygy," the unfortunate Dr. Godfrey, a previously well-respected pediatrician, finds a mob on his front step. In the McMartin case, teachers and day-care providers at the upper-class McMartin Preschool, considered a premiere establishment

TRIVIA BUSTER 14

Easy Stuff: *Take a single point for each correct answer.*

1. How did Comity, New Hampshire, describe itself?
2. What caught fire at Boom's funeral?
3. Who does the Ouija board claim Brenda is going to marry?
4. What macabre "present" does Detective Angela White find on her doorstep?
5. What unusual item ended up in Scott's chest?

Tougher Trivia: *These are two-pointers all the way.*

6. Which high school did the kids attend?
7. What did Mulder and Detective White claim to see in the burns on Jay De Boom's chest?
8. Who—for a price—handed out astrological advice?
9. What was buried in the pediatrician's briefcase?
10. When were Margi and Terri born?

by both its clients and its competition, were the targets. Before the McMartin trial ended, staff at twenty-one other facilities for young children had been accused. So were housekeepers, noncustodial parents, mayors, grandparents, public-school teachers, cops, and neighbors. Like Dr. Godfrey, the accused are usually longtime residents; few have any history of criminal activity, certainly no prior connection to pedophilia or satanism!

Though *The X-Files* enjoys a well-deserved reputation for twisting reality—and scaring the daylights out of its audience in the process—even those warped storytellers would be hard pressed to top the real charges brought during the "Satanic Day-Care Era" that began with McMartin and has yet to really disappear. According to charges brought in the McMartin trial, in between wandering about in the black robes, tending the red or black candles, and figuring out new ways to incorporate pentagrams into the decor, McMartin workers killed a horse *bare-handed*, took children off to car washes where they were flagrantly molested, or carted them off to "underground tunnels" to participate in satanic rituals. The bones of small animals, sacrificed during these rites, supposedly filled a massive pit deeper than the children themselves. And if all the children who were supposedly involved in the "naked movie-star games" performed all the sexual acts described in the statements and complaints, the sheer weight of film could have filled another facility. Some of the children even made statements about teachers who didn't begin working there until *after* the children graduated to public schools!

ANSWERS:

1. "The Perfect Harmony City."
2. His coffin.
3. Satan.
4. A box containing dead flowers and her cat's collar.
5. A garage-door spring.
6. Grover Cleveland Alexander.
7. A horned beast.
8. Zirinka.
9. The remains of Mr. Tippy, a fourteen-year-old Lhasa apso.
10. January 12, 1979.

YOUR SCORE _____

The makings of
a cosmic cocktail

One wonders when these industrious workers found time to make the peanut butter sandwiches or mock up all the arts and crafts required to keep parents blindly ignorant of any "irregularities" in their children's play programs. . . .

However, regardless of the apparent absurdity of the claims, parents and law enforcement weren't going to be seen to take any chances. In a pretrial phase that makes O.J.'s courtroom appearance look like a cameo, investigators and lawyers spent *eighteen months* determining that they simply didn't have enough evidence even to charge five of the preschool teachers.

Not only did no one find the pit of animal bones (mass graves, despite their size, seem notoriously hard to find), no one found the tunnels, robes, candles, or "secret rooms." Not surprisingly, investigators on the other cases couldn't find the remains of woodland altars or slaughtered children. Most telling, however, was the *lack* of physical evidence among the children themselves. Some of the acts described for investigators could never have been carried out without causing serious physical harm to the children. Yet in the McMartin case and others, the youngsters, on examination, proved to be completely sound, unmarked by any trauma whatsoever. Certainly no sexual abuse was evident.

The "evidence" admitted in an effort to have Peggy Boccie and her son Ray, the supposed horse-killer, held over never seemed particularly strong either. In the 1980s—but reminiscent of the witch trials of the 1680s!—Ray Boccie was asked if he'd ever engaged in premarital affairs. His dislike of underwear in torrid California became a crucial point in the prosecutor's case. His subscription to *Playboy* came up some forty times—despite its million-plus circulation, which indicates the legally available publication remains popular in quite a few quarters. The real capper, however, clearly indicative of a criminal mindset, seems to have been his interest in that eighties rage, pyramid power.

All charges against all former employees of the McMartin Preschool were eventually dropped, but not before taxpayers doled out some $15 million in a seven-year-long trial. Not before the McMartins' business and reputations were ruined. Not before their employees lost several life savings to lawyers' fees. Not before one couple lost their children to Child Services and foster care and spent the next two years trying to get them back. And not before dozens of children were apparently coerced into reworking memories and submitting to hours of interrogation and "therapy" better described as mental and physical torture.

Given the ridiculous nature of the atrocities claimed, everything from being taken away aboard spaceships to being branded, how could the charges have gained any credence in the first place? Clearly, Ray Boccie couldn't have brought a horse into the preschool without attracting some notice. So how could reports that he'd murdered it with his bare hands, a herculean task in itself, be taken seriously?

According to sociologists and the FBI's investigators, the 1980s, and the 1990s for that matter, provided uniquely rich soil for fear and paranoia, especially for concerns about children and "New Age" practices.

In the early eighties, divorce rates more than doubled, marriage was down, cohabitation was up. Children—and their parents—found themselves in new, frightening situations. Real and perceived abandonment, custody fights, abductions, and, unfortunately, genuine abuse spiraled upward, quickly becoming dominant social ills. Outside care for children was still new, and parental guilt ran high.

About the same time, "counselors," "therapists," and "intervention specialists" became media personalities. Whether the interviewee held a degree, was espousing the unproven theories of his latest book, or was the sole proponent of a new "therapeutical" exercise didn't seem important. One "expert," Dr. Harvey Klaus, received his doctorate in six weeks from a now-defunct church while working as a cafeteria cleaner. He managed to work his sideline, as a special advisor on devil worship to the FBI, into no less than forty-three televised interviews.

Incidentally, the FBI has never heard of Dr. Klaus and certainly has no record of ever having consulted him on anything. Unfortunately, not all clients were as discriminating as the FBI, and scores of unlicensed therapists proliferated across the United States. The idea of standardized evaluations went out the window when everyone was free to indulge his own method.

Religion, once the territory of white-steepled buildings behind equally white picket fences, encountered the New Age and hosts of new sects, some cults, and a great number of "free thinkers"; and neo-whatevers appeared as the population struggled to squeeze old religions into modern lifestyles. Women's advocacy, holistic health, and even the Green movements were drawn into the mix, producing, among other things, "niche" religions designed more along the lines of a Twelve-Step program than traditional worship. And, of course, in supporting and "protecting" their niche clientele, these new groups faced an old problem: Anything approaching a secret society invites speculation, usually negative speculation.

Two books purporting to expose and define the true nature of the occult religions exploded into a rash of conspiracy theories. Mike Warnke, author of *The Satan Seller*, claimed to have learned from personal experience and involvement that Satanists were a "deep and widespread organization, operating not only in the U.S., but all over the world." About that time, *Michelle Remembers*, supposedly a genuine account of one woman's recovery from childhood satanic ritual abuse, also appeared on bookstore shelves. Both books detailed, in gory and lurid detail, events that the authors portrayed as practically everyday occurrences. Of the SRA cases reported since their publication, few deviate in any significant way from the events in these two books. As Scully noted in "Syzygy," the statements since then are "almost cliché." Of course, some claim the similarities, like those among UFO abductees, are the result of the authenticity of the accounts, not a lack of diversity among the participants.

So prevalent did belief become in some form of satanic ritual abuse, and in satanic crimes ranging from desecration of Judeo-Christian places of worship to the wholesale slaughter of priests, that despite a lack of forensic evidence, the FBI eventually decided to carry out its own investigation.

The typical satanic-ritual-abuse reports would be familiar to any X-Phile, and quickly became familiar to investigators:

—Young teenage girl, virgin and beautiful, impregnated during a satanic ritual, is forcibly delivered of her nearly term baby, forced to ritually kill the child and then to cannibalize its heart as cult members watch. The remains, of no further value to cultists, get dumped into a mass garbage grave.

—Preschool child, usually in an out-of-home care situation, mentions a "new game," a secret new game. Under practices including hypnosis, regression therapy, and "playacting," bizarre tales emerge. Adults in hooded robes lay the naked child on an altar, paint it with blood or bloody symbols, conduct a "black mass," and either kill it ritually or actually, often after the slaughter of some small animals or after one of any number of sexual acts with the child itself. The body, or bodies, is disposed of in a mass grave.

Unfortunately, despite the forensic evidence that should be available to investigators after such elaborate rituals, people like Supervisory Special Agent Kenneth Lanning, of the FBI's Behavioral Sciences Unit, have yet to find so much as a drip of wax after investigating some 300 alleged incidents. It's only reasonable to expect that violent murders, involving upwards of a score of accessories to the crimes and that require hours to complete, would leave evidence.

Even if no physical evidence turned up, it's human nature for people to talk, to argue within any group, to have members of a group leave. Apparently, Satanists are an incredibly loyal group; certainly no one has ever brought forward reliable eyewitness testimony to any confirmed abuse or murder. None of the "baby breeders" were noticeably pregnant to anyone who knew them. None of them went to authorities in the long months of their pregnancies. None of them disappeared long enough to explain an unnoticed pregnancy. Even the Mafia and the CIA, arguably two of the most covert organizations in the United States, leave some sort of trail, yet Satanists, supposedly committing hundreds of crimes, don't even cause a blip in the sales of candles and black cloth.

While a lack of evidence might be explainable by really careful crooks, or by truly sloppy investigators, SRA is frequently undermined by *contrary* evidence, evidence tending to disprove the claim. Adelle Aiktins, one of the many "ritual survivors" who came to light in 1987, presented the death of her older brother as evidence of her family's involvement in a satanic cult that systematically bred children for ritual murder. Her brother, though hard to locate at a moment's notice, wasn't dead, and only nominally missing. To be excessively generous, since he did serve aboard an American destroyer, his address did change from moment to moment.

The FBI report never claimed that occult-related crimes didn't occur, but it seriously questioned the authenticity of the few cases that did seem to fit the SRA parameters. A self-proclaimed Satanist, Richard Kasso, did, without a doubt, kill his best friend. Some of the accoutrements of Satanism were present. A ritual of some type had apparently been enacted. But Kasso acted *alone*; there was no cult. Kasso's effects included a copy of a horror novel with some broad descriptions of a black mass, which Kasso appears to have acted out, but neither Kasso nor the author came even remotely close to an authentic ritual. A British case, which at first seemed to satisfy the conditions for satanic ritual abuse, failed miserably when the perpetrators admitted to having no knowledge of occultism, much less Satanism. Their sex killing of a young boy had been couched in terms of a ritual to force them to hold off killing, something which numerous murderers have claimed increases the pleasure when the desire is finally fulfilled.

Finally, though, there is fairly widespread belief in the idea that thousands of children go missing annually. Crime statistics, independently gathered, prove that isn't the case. Certainly, the 340 children currently listed as missing don't come anywhere close to the approximately 50,000 deaths required to satisfy the reported cases of infant or child satanic sacrifice. The whereabouts of most missing children are determined within twelve months—usually in the possession of a noncustodial parent; and though some children are indeed tragic victims of random violence, only one case appears to border on the satanic.

It would be hard to deny that violence is an increasingly prominent feature of American life, and people are notoriously inventive in finding new methods of inflicting pain on one another, but neither syzygy nor SRA is responsible.

eXtras:

Syzygy: a. a pair of things, especially a pair of opposites; b. or, from astronomy, either of two opposing points in the orbit of a heavenly body, specifically of the moon, at which it is in conjunction with or in opposition to the sun; c. or, from biology, the conjunction of two organisms without loss of identity.

X

Dana Wheeler-Nicholson, who portrays Detective White in this episode, accompanied David Duchovny to the 1996 Golden Globe Awards. He recently split from his previous date for the occasion, longtime girlfriend and *X-File* guest star Perrey Reeves. Suzanne Lanza was his companion at the Screen Actors Guild Awards in March. Unlike Fox Mulder, David Duchovny doesn't appear to have any difficulty finding a companionable woman for an evening out.

Dana Wheeler-Nicholson

Code Name: ''GROTESQUE''

CASE SUMMARY:

When Special Agent William Patterson, stern hero of the Behavioral Sciences Unit and Mulder's former mentor, calls in his wayward student, the tension between them is palpable and—in Scully's opinion—unlikely to contribute to the resolution of a case already cluttered with ''demons'' and ''gargoyles.'' Neither Mulder nor Scully, however, is prepared for the mental cesspool Patterson asks Mulder to ''get inside.''

EYEWITNESS STATEMENT:

''Well, from what I hear, there were a lot of men who . . . A lot of men joined the FBI because they wanted to *be* him.''

—Special Agent Dana Scully

DEEP BACKGROUND:

Joining the Ranks

Few X-Philes could watch three seasons of *The X-Files*, three seasons of near-heroic quests, extraordinary successes, and dismal failures, without, at some point, wondering how the average Joe (or Jane) is admitted to the FBI's tight ranks. Even with bad press from incidents like Waco, and with lawyers casting more aspersions against its operatives and methodology than confetti at a wedding, the title Special Agent of the Federal Bureau of Investigation still carries a certain mystique. The heady days when the FBI seemed about to run out of fugitives for its "Ten Most Wanted," the odd romance that touched both cops and crooks during the "Gangster Era," and the agents' resilient image as crime fighters in suits and ties combined to create a very different professional portrait from that of the average street cop.

That difference was—and is—more than cosmetic.

Unlike most police forces, whose job is to prevent or prosecute crimes, the FBI is primarily a fact-finding body. Its scope includes the investigation of matters that, in all likelihood, will never be part of any prosecution. In fact, criminal prosecution falls *outside* FBI jurisdiction. Though millions of bits of information and evidence pass through its offices yearly, every scrap is destined for SED (Someone Else's Desk), including its "parent" organization, the Department of Justice. Whether employees fall into the special-agent or support designation is almost immaterial. *All* FBI personnel, in some way or other, contribute to the accumulation of information and evidence that other law enforcement personnel need to make their cases.

While its criminal investigations garner media attention, reappear as movies, and inspire television shows, a considerable percentage of the FBI's resources has nothing to do with traditional criminals— unless you include politicians in that group. Hundreds of agents and support personnel plow through stacks of foreign counterintelligence, while others handle routine background checks, evaluate evidence for civil cases, and, of course, teach!

Not surprisingly, such diverse activities require a broad range of talent; and, unlike most federal employees, FBI personnel are among the "excepted service," outside the usual civil service population, and are recruited directly instead of through the Office of Personnel Management. The Director's discretion extends to hiring, discipline, and promotions. Excellence can be rewarded much more quickly than in other branches of service. Service in the Bureau, in any of its positions (generally broken down into administrative, clerical, technical, professional, and other), is challenging—and incredibly competitive. Hundreds of hopefuls contact the Bureau's field offices each year, applying for a limited number of behind-the-scenes support positions, or for the more public position of special agent.

For those who receive serious consideration, a gauntlet of tests and investigations await. Rigorous psychological testing, aptitude examinations, interviews, and written exams are just the beginning. The FBI likes to know everything about its personnel, and it has the resources to discover just about anything. Regular background/personal investigations of prospective employees include a rummage through the applicant's credit and criminal histories, chats with current personal and professional contacts, interviews with ten or more years' worth of neighbors and employers, frequent drug testing, a physical exam worthy of any boot camp, and, in many cases, voluntary submission to lie-detector examinations. All that just for the big interview!

Only after candidates survive the initial checks and exams are they considered for positions in the ranks of FBI special agents. Basic requirements are fairly simple. The applicant must be a U.S. citizen, in good health, between the ages of twenty-three and thirty-seven. Not so bad. The next requirement, a minimum of a bachelor's degree (four-year program) from a college or university, begins to separate FBI special agents from most municipal cops and state troopers. So does the sixteen-week program at the FBI Academy in Quantico. In addition to a demanding fitness program, personal defense classes, and firearms

TRIVIA BUSTER 15

Easy Stuff: *Just one point for each correct answer.*

1. How was Agent Nemhauser's hand injured?
2. What critter startled Scully in Mostow's studio?
3. What was hidden inside the clay sculptures?
4. Who checked out the missing murder weapon last?
5. Whose cell phone did Mulder find in a coat discarded in Mostow's studio?

Tougher Trivia: *Take two points for each of these.*

6. What detail of his past did Mostow "forget" to include on his American immigration forms?
7. Who arranged for Mulder to be assigned to this particular case?
8. In what investigative section was Patterson Mulder's immediate superior?
9. What did Agent Sheherlis refer to as "redwop"?
10. In which evidence room was material property for this case, FBI #14361, stored?

training, prospective agents carry a heavy course load of academic and technical/investigative subjects. The Bureau once claimed to employ the "cream of law enforcement," and even today, you'd be hard pressed to find better-prepared operatives.

The support personnel who fill professional, administrative, technical, clerical, craft, trade, and maintenance positions across the country are no slouches either. While a high school diploma is the minimum educational requirement, most employees also hold bachelor's—and more—degrees or technical certificates, and as a group, the FBI's support staff represents an incredible body of work experience. Among the many positions within the support staff are administrative assistants, budget analysts, carpenters, clerks, computer programmers, data entry operators, electricians, electronics technicians, engineering technicians, intelligence research specialists, laboratory technicians, language specialists, paralegals, secretaries, and writers. Not satisfied with any of those? The full list includes more than a hundred job descriptions, and the Bureau's support staff is encouraged to train in new fields.

Most government jobs come with a set of built-in benefits, and the FBI is no exception. Monetary remuneration meets and usually exceeds similar positions in the private sector. Support-staff pay scales fall within the GS-4 to GS-9 categories; in specialty areas, exceptions have been made to normal grade levels in recognition of special education, work experience, or prior government service.

ANSWERS:

1. John Mostow bit him.
2. A black cat.
3. The dismembered remains of the victims.
4. Mulder.
5. Agent Nemhauser's.
6. That he'd been institutionalized in an insane asylum for nearly a decade.
7. Agent Patterson.
8. ISU, the Investigative Services Unit.
9. "Powder" spelled backward, a special (fluorescent) dusting powder for print work.
10. Evidence room L-7 at FBI headquarters.

YOUR SCORE _____

Special agents bring home the GS-10 to GS-13 rates, with agents in supervisory, management, and executive positions qualifying for the GS-14 and GS-15 scales or, in a few cases, Senior Executive Service payouts. All special agents also qualify for . . . overtime.

The FBI used to have a second, less frequently discussed reputation as well, as the most-likely-to-discriminate-on-the-basis-of-just-about-anything. It wasn't long ago that the only women in the FBI were typists and the only blacks were drivers for the Bureau's higher-ups. It went almost without saying that there were no disabled agents or support staff. That's changing. At the end of 1995, 823 disabled employees had joined the ranks of the FBI—and they weren't token employees. Much like their fellow agents, they're divided equally between FBI HQ and the field. While men, white men, are still the largest group of employees, the percentages of working agents who are members of minority groups are very much in line with the percentages of those applying. The FBI has come a long way, baby. And, for many, it presents a very attractive career option.

eXtras:

You Say "Gargoyle," I Say "Grotesque" Like "gargle," "gargoyle" comes from *gargouille*, the French word for "waterspout" and "drainpipe," and with good reason if you know that a gargoyle can only be a gargoyle if it spits water. Before PVC eaves, troughs, and drainpipes, most gutters, like most large buildings, were made of stone. Gargoyles were simply decorative predecessors to the modern downspout.

The fanciful, free-standing statuary featured throughout this episode is, as the title clearly states, more properly called "grotesque."

To think that the grotesque is comparatively useless, however, depends on how much of the "pagan" still echoes in your psyche. Although both gargoyles and grotesques decorated those most Christian of edifices, the gothic churches and cathedrals, they were "political hangovers," something of an olive branch extended to local populations who weren't quite ready to abandon all their old ways when they accepted Christianity. As long as the locals weren't actually worshipping the carvings, they were allowed. And since the sculptures had never been idols, there was no reason for dissension over them.

So why the imaginative shapes?

In a sense, they were spiritual scarecrows. Just as a person might prop a straw man in his garden to frighten crows, an ugly statue was thought to keep demons and devils, with their bad luck, away from homes or special places.

X

Wondering how Mulder and Scully can afford a wardrobe that Chanel or Hugo Boss would be proud of? Or how Skinner manages to look so devastatingly well dressed? Most FBI agents fall into the GS-12 range on the pay scale, about $46,000 when the *The X-Files* opened in 1994, and average a further 25 percent under a section called Administratively Uncontrollable Overtime for a tidy total of nearly $60,000 per year. Assistant Directors, considerably farther up the scale, begin at $118,512 and, yes, they qualify for overtime too. But if wardrobe is a function of income, whoever pays The Cigarette-Smoking Man is akin to Scrooge!

X-REFERENCE:

Inside the FBI

Though the Federal Bureau of Investigation employs the vast majority of its personnel at the Washington Bureau, FBI headquarters, which is also home base for our favorite fictional agents, its entire structure is designed to move people and resources to its field offices as efficiently as possible, while facilitating the flow of information back to the central databases.

To handle that flood of bodies and data, the FBI settled into distinct divisions years ago, nine divisions and three offices to be exact, all based in the Washington, D.C., offices. Each of the divisions (Inspection, Legal Counsel, Identification, Information Management, Technical Service, Intelligence, Laboratory, Training, and Criminal Investigative Division) is headed by an Assistant Director.

The three offices are headed by executives with varying titles. An Inspector in Charge manages the Office of Public and Congressional Affairs, and the Office of the General Counsel is headed by the General Counsel. The Office of Equal Employment Opportunity Affairs is administered by the Equal Employment Opportunity Officer.

From this central processing area, the Bureau's 20,000-plus agents and staff provide program initiatives and support services to fifty-six field offices, the four hundred suboffices called resident agencies, and the twenty-two Legal Attaché and Legal Liaison Officers heading the foreign liaison posts. The last segment of the resource/information loop consists of the four specialized field installations. Through that hierarchy, nearly 11,000 special agents work as a team to investigate everything from basic bank robberies to the cutting edge of computer crime. A further 14,000 permanent employees support that effort through an incredibly diverse spectrum of professional, clerical, craft, trade, administrative, technical, and maintenance services. Following the chain of command leads directly back to the Deputy Director and, of course, the Director.

Moving down the ladder, toward the level of individual agents, leads to the Deputy Assistant Directors, who oversee general operations. These follow commonsensical branches into sections and, from there, into units, the most specialized of working groups. A two-person operation like the fictional X-Files would likely fall rather neatly into the unit designation. Considering the hierarchical distance between an Assistant Director and one of the working units in his division, Skinner's regular involvement with two agents who prefer to act first and report later is rather exceptional.

Fortunately for real-life agents, who seldom function as independently as Mulder would like to, the fifty-six field offices are located rather conveniently across the entire country. With the exception of the New York City and Washington, D.C., offices, which are run by an Assistant Director in Charge (ADIC), each field office is run by a Special Agent in Charge (SAC) supported by Assistant Special Agents in Charge (ASACs) and, in general, by Squad Supervisors, who manage the investigative side, and Office Services Managers, who handle the administrative tasks.

Depending on the amount and type of crime within a field office's area, a floating number of resident agencies with appropriate personnel and resources is established. A resident agency can consist of a single agent or upwards of a score of employees. Big agencies rate a Supervisory Senior Resident Agent, who handles communication between the agency personnel and the field office.

Masses of information pass from all these offices to the FBI's specialized field installations. Two Regional Computer Support Centers (RCSCs) are found in Pocatello, Idaho, and Fort Monmouth, New Jersey. Two Information Technology Centers (ITCs) operate out of Butte, Montana, and Savannah, Georgia. The ITCs provide information services to support field investigative and administrative operations. In addition, the FBI provides support for the National Drug Intelligence Center (NDIC) in Johnstown, Pennsylvania. The NDIC collects and consolidates intelligence on drug trafficking from law enforcement and other official users, and is overseen by the U.S. Department of Justice.

In the first three seasons, Scully and Mulder hit state after state, even venturing into the wilds of Alaska and sneaking off to Puerto Rico. On the odd occasion when the trail led outside America proper *The X-Files* preferred to allow audiences to assume their fictional heroes were acting independently, even unofficially, instead of digging into the FBI's overseas offices. Should Mulder or Scully ever cross the border on legitimate business, a well-established and absolutely authentic system of international offices could certainly lend a few more exotic locales to the story lines. Of course, the mandatory cooperation of the foreign government might make life as difficult overseas as at home.

Still, with the FBI becoming increasingly involved in investigating international criminal activity (and higher ratings making bigger budgets a possibility!), we may eventually see Mulder and Scully struggling with the native lingos; figuring out which side of the road to drive on; and generally getting lost faster than they would at home while tracking the international links of the mysterious Consortium. At which point, introducing the talented people running the Legal Attaché offices would certainly add yet another touch of reality to *The X-Files'* more fantastic plots.

Reporting to the International Relations Branch of the Criminal Investigative Division at FBI HQ, the Legal Attachés monitor the pulse of their regions and provide considerable support to their own and visiting agents. International Relations also establishes liaisons with the Executive Branch, Interpol, any foreign police or security officers based in D.C. (such as visiting Scotland Yard officers), and American-based national law enforcement associations.

There are Legal Attaché offices located in twenty-two countries around the world, usually officially assigned to the American embassies in those countries. Special agents working abroad generally fall into one of the Legal Attaché, Deputy Legal Attaché, or Assistant Legal Attaché job descriptions. The exceptions are those special agents working out of Honolulu, Miami, and San Juan who are liaison officers.

Until Mulder and Scully take their show on the road, however,

they'll be heavily dependent on the assistance of their more local colleagues, so even if they're careful whom they trust, it helps to know
where to find them.

Albany, New York	Albuquerque, New Mexico
Anchorage, Alaska	Atlanta, Georgia
Baltimore, Maryland	Birmingham, Alabama
Boston, Massachusetts	Buffalo, New York
Charlotte, North Carolina	Chicago, Illinois
Cincinnati, Ohio	Cleveland, Ohio
Columbia, South Carolina	Dallas, Texas
Denver, Colorado	Detroit, Michigan
El Paso, Texas	Honolulu, Hawaii
Houston, Texas	Indianapolis, Indiana
Jackson, Mississippi	Jacksonville, Florida
Kansas City, Missouri	Knoxville, Tennessee
Las Vegas, Nevada	Little Rock, Arkansas
Los Angeles, California	Louisville, Kentucky
Memphis, Tennessee	North Miami Beach, Florida
Milwaukee, Wisconsin	Minneapolis, Minnesota
Mobile, Alabama	Newark, New Jersey
New Haven, Connecticut	New Orleans, Louisiana
New York, New York	Norfolk, Virginia
Oklahoma City, Oklahoma	Omaha, Nebraska
Philadelphia, Pennsylvania	Phoenix, Arizona
Pittsburgh, Pennsylvania	Portland, Oregon
Richmond, Virginia	Sacramento, California
St. Louis, Missouri	Salt Lake City, Utah
San Antonio, Texas	San Diego, California
San Francisco, California	San Juan, Puerto Rico
Seattle, Washington	Springfield, Illinois
Tampa, Florida	Washington, D.C.

eXtras:

The FBI's total annual funding for all operations, salaries, and ex-
penses is approximately $2.2 billion.

Code Name: "PIPER MARU"

CASE SUMMARY:

When Mulder's knack of connecting disjointed bits of information kicks in, he suspects a link between the mysterious *Talapus*, which he believes brought up a crashed UFO, and a second ship, the French *Piper Maru*, whose crew is dying of radiation exposure. Scully, however, is making connections of her own, which lead her back to her own childhood and her sister's murder.

EYEWITNESS STATEMENT:

"You're in the basement because they're *afraid* of you, of your re-lentlessness—and because they know that they could drop you in the middle of the desert and tell you the truth is out there and you'd ask them for a shovel."

—Special Agent Dana Scully

TRIVIA BUSTER 16

Easy Stuff: *One point for each correct answer.*

1. From what illness did the French sailors suffer?
2. How much pay-phone change did the shooter supposedly want from the waitress?
3. What former partner did Mulder escort back to the U.S.?
4. To what city did Mulder take Flight 621?
5. How much time passes between Melissa Scully's death and this episode?

Tougher Trivia: *You'll have to earn your two points for these.*

6. What was the name of Johansen's sub?
7. In front of what monument did Mr. and Mrs. Gauthier have their photo taken?
8. How does Skinner like his steak?
9. What was Gauthier's first name?
10. What were the call numbers of the downed plane?

Gillian Anderson at the 2nd Annual SAG Awards

ANSWERS:

1. Radiation sickness.
2. $1.75.
3. Agent Krycek.
4. Hong Kong.
5. Five months.

6. *Zeus Faber*.
7. The Eiffel Tower.
8. Medium rare.
9. Bernard.
10. JTTO 111470.

YOUR SCORE _____

At the Center of the Action I

The Woman:

GILLIAN ANDERSON

VITAL STATISTICS

DOB:	August 9, 1968
Place of Birth:	Chicago, Illinois
Height:	5'3"
Hair:	Blond, colored auburn
Eyes:	Hazel
Parents:	Rosemary and Edward
Siblings:	Two
Marital Status:	Married to Clyde Klotz
Children:	One, Piper, a daughter who was born during the early part of the second season's filming, on September 25, 1994. Creative filming allowed Anderson's real-life and fictional personas to remain firmly separate.

EDUCATIONAL INFORMATION

- Attended Fountain Elementary, Grand Rapids, Michigan.
- Graduated from City High, Grand Rapids, Michigan, 1986.
- Attended DePaul University's prestigious Goodman Theater School, graduating with a Bachelor of Fine Arts.
- Studied at the National Theater of Great Britain at Cornell University, Ithaca, New York.

PROFESSIONAL INFORMATION

Anderson's acting ambitions began back in Grand Rapids, where she became involved in community theater. While at DePaul University, she earned a role in *The Turning* but moved east—not west—at graduation, choosing to pursue a career in theater instead of film. Three years later she'd appeared in *The Philanthropist* at the Long Wharf Theater and won a Theater World Award for her performance in a production of Alan Ayckbourne's *Absent Friends*, an impressive achievement in a role for which she had only a few weeks to study.

A dip into television with *Home Fires Burning*, a talking book version of *Exit to Eden*, and an episode of *Class of '96* later, she was willing to consider taking an episodic role. The character of Dana Scully, a bright woman who'd sacrificed nothing of her femininity to a demanding career, had an irresistible appeal.

Chris Carter had already decided Anderson was made for the role, and despite some "questions" from the network—they suggested casting someone "taller, leggier, skinnier, [and] with a lot more chest"—Gillian Anderson was cast as Scully.

At the Second Annual Screen Actors Guild Awards, where actors honor the best among them, Gillian Anderson was awarded the hefty statue as the best actress in a dramatic television program. Considering that Anderson hadn't actually believed the show would run beyond its original half season of preliminary episodes, had no experience of the daily grind of television production, and wasn't prepared for the mental strain of attempting to appear "fresh" for take after take after take, she's already displayed a level of professionalism others in the field could learn from.

OTHER RESIDENCES

As a young woman, Gillian Anderson traveled widely, following her father, also an actor, from Puerto Rico to London to Grand Rapids and Chicago. She has since lived in New York City and Los Angeles and currently makes her home in North Vancouver, British Columbia, Canada.

FAVORITE EPISODES

Not surprisingly, those that give her the scope to really show off her talents, "Beyond the Sea" and "Irresistible." Given that criteria, "Revelations" from season three is another natural.

EARLY AMBITIONS

Archaeologist
Marine Biologist

The Character:

DANA KATHERINE SCULLY

PERSONNEL DOSSIER

#121-627-161

Name:	**Dana Katherine Scully**
Position:	Special Agent, Department of Justice, Federal Bureau of Investigation
Currently Assigned:	The X-Files
FBI ID#:	2317-616
Contact #'s:	(Home) 202-555-6431
	(Cellular) 202-555-3564

PERSONAL INFORMATION

DOB:	February 23, 1964
	(Later changed to November 21, 1964, in the episodes "Nisei" and "731.")
Height:	5'2"
Hair:	Red
Eyes:	Blue/Green/Hazel
Marital Status:	Single/Never Married/No Dependents
Parents:	Father—Captain Jim Scully (deceased)
	Mother—Margaret Scully
Siblings:	Two brothers (one older, one younger) are both unremarkable. Older sister, Melissa, known to entertain certain "New Age" philosophies, died from a single gunshot wound to the head. The incident occurred at the residence of Agent Scully and has been linked to habitual criminal Louis Cardinal, now deceased.
In Case of Emergency:	Notify—Margaret Scully (mother)
	Religious Affiliation—Roman Catholic
	(N.B.: A Living Will is on file.)

EDUCATIONAL INFORMATION

Agent Scully came to the Bureau after completing an undergraduate degree in physics from the University of Maryland before completing a medical degree.

Graduated FBI Training Academy, Quantico, in 1992.

(N.B. Maintained open relationship with Instructor/Special Agent Jack Willis during training.)

WORK HISTORY (CHRONOLOGICAL)

Completed Medical Residency
Assigned Quantico Training Facility, Instructor
Assigned X-Files, Field Agent (March 6, 1992)
Reassigned Quantico Training Facility, Instructor
Reassigned X-Files, Field Agent

SUPERVISORY NOTES (CHRONOLOGICAL)

1. It is the hope of this department that Agent Scully, coming from, and to all appearances more dedicated to, a more "traditional" scientific approach, will be able to properly assess the quantitative value of Agent Mulder's work, while observing that agent's general deportment and state of mind.

2. During a recent interview, our debriefing agent had cause to believe that assigning Agent Scully to the X-Files may not have been as well advised as originally thought. While the agent continues, in general, to adhere to the criminal investigative techniques outlined as optimal by this office, a tendency to "open-mindedness" has been observed.

3. Following a job-related abduction by Duane Barry (a known psychotic whom we suspect to have been working with an accomplice), Agent Scully received treatment for her injuries and was encouraged to discuss the incident with the Bureau's in-house psychiatric staff. As such appointments are covered by doctor-patient confidentiality, no information regarding those sessions is available at this time. Reports of her field capability continue to support her decision to return to her previous duties, but constant reviews of her case files will be continued for the present time.
(N.B. Until such time as Agent Scully is able to compile a description of the events of her abduction, X-File #73317 must remain open.)

4. Following the events on the Two Grey Hills reserve, which may have resulted in the death of her partner, it is the recommendation of the Office of Professional Conduct that Special Agent Dana Scully be given a mandatory leave of absence until the full details of her misconduct can be calculated. This summary action is justified under the OPC Articles of Review, and Agent Scully will complete her suspension of duty without pay or benefits due to the nature of her insubordination and the direct disobedience of her superior agents.

5. Agent Scully has been reinstated. While her complicity in her partner's activities is evident, her involvement in his disappearance, in his unauthorized investigations, or in his insubordination cannot be assessed at this time. Her involvement in his death is, of course, moot.

6. Following the intervention of the Japanese Diplomatic Corps, Special Agent Scully and Special Agent Mulder have been officially denied permission to continue any investigation of the death of Steven Zinnzser.

7. At the request of Special Agent Patterson, investigation into a possible attempt by Agent Scully to obstruct justice and a federal agent, Special Agent Fox Mulder, in the performance of his duties has begun.

8. Investigation was dropped due to lack of evidence and special circumstances.

9. An appeal lodged by Special Agent Dana Scully, and seconded by Assistant Director Walter S. Skinner, to continue the investigation into the death of Melissa Scully has been received. It will be handled along with other paperwork of its type.

10. Following a refusal by her partner, Agent Fox Mulder, Agent Scully sought approval to divulge information to writer Jose Chung, and such request, having no bearing on secured information, has been granted. Liaison is to be through the Bureau's Public Relations Department and to be in accordance with the Freedom of Information Act provisions.

eXtras:

A Little More Name-Dropping . . . Sailors and airmen have been naming their boats and planes since they first floated or flew, usually after the women in their lives. The X-crew continued the tradition in "Piper Maru." They named the French boat after Gillian Anderson's daughter and paid a tribute to the mother with "Drop Dead Red."

Code Name: "APOCRYPHA"

CASE SUMMARY:

The links Mulder sensed lurking behind the events surrounding the *Piper Maru* begin to come together as Scully connects the shooting of Assistant Director Skinner to that of her sister while Mulder tracks the path of the elusive wreckage they both believe is responsible for deaths stretching back to 1953. When former agent Alex Krycek turns up once again, it's difficult *not* to believe the connection will come full circle.

EYEWITNESS STATEMENT:

"Listen to me! Anger is a luxury that you cannot afford right now. If you're angry, you're going to make a mistake. And these people will take advantage of that. You've seen how they operate."
—**Assistant Director Walter Skinner**

TRIVIA BUSTER 17

The first five are easy, but the rest are two-pointers all the way.

1. Where was Skinner when he was shot?
2. What was written on Krycek's key?
3. How was the FBI able to secure genetic information on Skinner's shooter?
4. What did Mulder believe the "alien" used to jump from person to person?
5. What piece of investigative equipment did Mulder use to recover a phone number?
6. What car rental company did Mulder use?
7. Which road are Krycek and Mulder so effectively forced off?
8. Which agent shows a romantic interest in Dana Scully?
9. Where did Skinner see his assailant before?
10. From what facility did The Lone Gunmen attempt to retrieve a package for Mulder?

At the Center of the Action II

The Man:

DAVID WILLIAM DUCHOVNY

VITAL STATISTICS

DOB:	August 7, 1960
Place of Birth:	New York City
Height:	6'
Hair:	Brown
Eyes:	Hazel
Identifying Mark:	Mole on right cheek
Parents:	Amram and Margaret Ducovny
Siblings:	Daniel (older), living in Los Angeles
	Laurie (younger), living in New York City
Marital Status:	Single and dating
Children:	None

EDUCATIONAL INFORMATION

- Collegiate Prep, Manhattan
- Princeton University, B.A.
- Yale University, M.A. (English), Ph.D. (unfinished); Dissertation: "Magic and Technology in Contemporary Poetry and Prose"
- The Actors Studio

PROFESSIONAL INFORMATION

Filmography

Working Girl, 1988
New Year's Day, 1989 (in which he appears nude)
Twin Peaks, 1990 (TV)
Bad Influence, 1990
Julia Has Two Lovers, 1991 (in which he appears nude)
Denial, 1991
Don't Tell Mom the Babysitter's Dead, 1991
The Rapture, 1991
Beethoven, 1992
Baby Snatcher, 1992 (TV)
Ruby, 1992
Chaplin, 1992
Red Shoe Diaries, 1992 (TV)
Venice/Venice, 1992
Kalifornia, 1993
Playing God, 1996

INTERESTS

Sports, both individual (jogging, swimming, and yoga) and team (basketball and baseball). Writing, including poetry. Music. Theater.

ANSWERS:

1. At a coffee shop.
2. C.I. 517.
3. With saliva—the "Hispanic Man" spit on Skinner.
4. Heavy diesel oil.
5. A pencil.
6. As in most episodes, Lariat Rent-A-Car.
7. County Road 512 in Maryland.
8. Agent Pendrell.
9. In a stairwell—just before Krycek stole the DAT tape.
10. Capital Ice—Maryland's finest skating wonderland.

YOUR SCORE _____

A rare smile from the man whose interview persona frequently comes across as self-absorbed or perennially depressed.

The Character:

FOX WILLIAM MULDER

PERSONNEL DOSSIER

#118-366-047

Name:	**Fox William Mulder**
Position:	Special Agent, Department of Justice, Federal Bureau of Investigation
Currently Assigned:	The X-Files
FBI Badge ID#:	JTTO 47101111
Contact #'s:	(Home) 202-555-0199

PERSONAL INFORMATION

DOB:	October 11, 1960 (Later changed to October 13, 1960, in the episodes "Nisei" and "731.")
Height:	6'
Hair:	Medium Brown
Eyes:	Hazel
Marital Status:	Single/Never Married/No Dependents
Parents:	Father—William Mulder (deceased/murdered) Mother—currently medically incompetent
Siblings:	One sister, Samantha T. Mulder, disappeared from the family home November 27, 1973. Whereabouts remain unknown.
In Case of Emergency:	Agent Dana Scully, Washington Bureau Religious Affiliation—Unknown

EDUCATIONAL INFORMATION

Agent Mulder graduated Oxford with a degree in psychology. Graduated high in his class, FBI Training Academy, Quantico.

WORK HISTORY (CHRONOLOGICAL)

Completed Psychology Residency
Assigned Violent Crimes Section, Behavioral Sciences Unit
Assigned X-Files, Field Agent
Assigned Intelligence Division, Communications
Reassigned X-Files, Field Agent

SUPERVISORY NOTES (CHRONOLOGICAL)

1. On the recommendation of his instructors, and in keeping with his graduate training, Agent Mulder has been assigned to the Behavioral Sciences Unit of the Violent Crimes Section.

2. An inquiry into the death of his former partner determined that Agent Mulder acted properly and was in no way responsible for the death of Agent Lamana.

3. A notation of exemplary service in the Props case has been added to this file.

4. At his own request, and with the consent of his superiors, Agent Mulder has undertaken the task of investigating some previously unsolved cases. It is anticipated that this is a temporary assignment to help clear a backlog, and that Agent Mulder will soon be returning to VCS.

5. As Agent Mulder shows no indication of returning to his previous assignment in the near future, an informal inquiry into the value of his present assignment will be instituted to determine if his skills might be better employed outside the X-Files.

6. Agent Dana Scully has been assigned to the X-Files and will be reporting directly to the administration.

7. Following some unorthodox investigations, it has been determined that Agent Mulder will be reassigned to a regular field position. (Transfer to Intelligence, Communications, and Surveillance.)

8. Under the direction of Assistant Director Skinner, both agents Mulder and Scully have returned to their pursuit of the X-Files. Duration of this assignment has yet to be specified.

9. This agent's involvement in the unauthorized and irregular activities of the Two Grey Hills Navajo reserve has been noted as further evidence of his inability to operate within the system. However, as his activities *were* unofficial, and could not be deemed illegal, no internal disciplinary action will be taken.

10. The Japanese Diplomatic Corps has filed formal requests for investigation into the actions of Agent Mulder in the wake of a string of deaths of Japanese personnel.

11. The requests on the part of the Japanese Diplomatic Corps have been dropped, no reason given.

12. Agent Mulder has formally declined to apply for a position in Special Agent Patterson's VCS unit.

13. Agent Mulder has formally declined to cooperate with writer Jose Chung. Request is being rerouted through Public Relations.

14. Despite some reservations by the OPC, Agent Mulder has accepted an invitation to appear at NICAP's AGM as the keynote speaker, his address loosely titled "The Case of Observer Credibility."

Yet More Science Bloopers!

- As the shooter didn't spit on Melissa Scully, where did the genetic material required to place him at that crime scene come from? In order to "match" DNA evidence, Agent Pendrell would have needed something to compare it to.
- The waitress must have been an attorney's dream witness. According to Scully, she'd already told them the shooter was "a male, probably in his forties, *with blood type B-positive.*" Not bad for an *eye*witness.

And Time Errors, Too!

"Krycek? Alex Krycek disappeared *five months* ago!"

Will Scully or Mulder realize that, while the Consortium may have lost track of Krycek five months ago, to Mulder and others, Krycek actually disappeared shortly after Scully's abduction—many months before? Will Mulder's talent for linking information tell him that The Cigarette-Smoking Man was in contact with Krycek *after* Scully's abduction—when Krycek was a wanted criminal?

Code Name: "PUSHER"

CASE SUMMARY:

The body count is rising swiftly, but with dozens of witnesses claiming the deaths were suicide, not murder, Mulder and Scully must track a charismatic killer who appears capable of "convincing" others to do *anything* he wants. Far from intimidating their quarry, the agents inspire him to new atrocities, gradually drawing both Scully and Mulder deeper into his intimate—and deadly—game.

EYEWITNESS STATEMENT:

"What do you need me to say, Mulder? That I believe that Modell is guilty of murder? I do! I'm just looking for an explanation a little more mundane than the 'whammy.' "

—Special Agent Dana Scully

DEEP BACKGROUND:

If I Could Make a Suggestion?

"It's like suddenly I was watching myself from across the room . . . doing these things! It's like he was with me, inside my head!"

—Holly

On a stage covered in the frosty mist of dry ice, glittering in the magical costumes most performance hypnotists affect, a man with dramatically cut sideburns and three layers of mascara increases the intensity of his gaze. Then he commands a woman to quack like a duck while waddling about in front of a crowd of several thousand.

She does.

Though chuckling loudly at the ridiculous picture the hapless victim cuts, the audience also shifts uneasily in its seats. After all, she didn't *seem* particularly gullible, no more likely than anyone else to spend hours believing her finger was stuck to the center of her forehead. That niggle of uncertainty about what apparently normal people could be made to do under hypnosis has inspired numerous films and a particularly effective episode of *The X-Files*, ''Pusher.'' While not hypnosis in the traditional version of the watch-spinning psychiatrist or the flamboyant stage hypnotist, Pusher's ability to play on his victims' hypersuggestibility is still a highly effective, if traditional, card in the horror writer's deck.

Despite years of study, science still can't completely explain how hypnosis works, what its limitations are, or why it affects some so powerfully and others not at all. Without those answers, it's impossible to completely rule out a menace like Pusher, or eliminate the doubt that we're safe from a quacking-clucking fate.

John Barrymore and Marion Marsh in *Svengali*

Even defining hypnosis proves difficult. Some researchers still believe it is an "altered state" of mind, requiring a careful setup, with the hypnotist clearly the dominant factor. Others see "hypnotic trances" as common occurrences, easily induced by the subjects themselves and independent of any hypnotic practitioner. Athletes frequently report a heightened awareness of their goals, surroundings, and abilities which they describe as "being in the zone." Basketball hoops appear huge. Balance beams feel as wide as city streets. Sprained muscles, torn ligaments, even broken bones cause no pain. Balance, muscle control, and dexterity measurably improve, all without the crystal-spinning agency of a hypnotist. Such practical applications of "altered states" of consciousness tend to support the theory that "hypnosis" and "self-hypnosis" are actually natural forms of perception that some people attain more easily than others.

Being "in the zone," however, isn't the stuff of horror films or X-Files, and that's where the role of the hypnotist becomes a necessary part of the plot. Obviously, no one would induce himself to perform

TRIVIA BUSTER 18

Easy Stuff: *Take a single point for each correct answer.*

1. What color was Deputy Scott Kerber's uniform?
2. How much should Pusher have netted from his bet with Mulder?
3. Who did Burst suggest was Modell's interior decorator?
4. Who put a size 7 heel print in the middle of Skinner's forehead?
5. Which flavor of "Carbo Boost" did Modell prefer?

Tougher Trivia: *These are two-pointers all the way.*

6. What magazine did Mulder figure Pusher would have stacked on the back of his toilet?
7. What did Pusher jokingly claim was inside his golf ball?
8. How was Collins injured?
9. What was Pusher's legal name?
10. Name the lobby guard who not only admitted Pusher, but inadvertently helped Scully find the implant in her neck in "731."

acts outside his normal, personal goals. To introduce the real fears, the possible loss of control, the notion of mental as well as physical force being brought to bear on us, pressures we couldn't withstand, the stuff that Chris Carter is so fond of saying will "scare the pants off us," requires a modern-day Svengali.

That hypnosis, the tool of Mesmer and Pusher, exists is undeniable. While some hypnotic subjects have been accused of colluding with their hypnotists to produce favorable results, even the most cooperative subjects wouldn't lie calmly under the surgeon's scalpel or the dentist's drill unless, as they claim, they "simply didn't feel any pain" under the effects of hypnosis. Nor could they control bleeding, lower their blood pressure, or alter their body temperature, all of which are well-documented events. That a suggestion alone could cause allergic reaction, blisters, and "sunburn" is incomprehensible to most of us. That similar suggestions could cure long-standing conditions like psoriasis or increase the number of white blood cells borders on the miraculous. Something is happening, but what and, more importantly, *how* are unknown.

If the mechanism allowing physical responses remains misunderstood, it's hardly surprising that mental responses are even less understood. The classic study asks a hypnotized subject to recall some detail apparently unrecoverable under standard conditions. Cases of eyewitnesses recalling license plate numbers, clock faces, where a criminal might have a mole, scar, or tattoo, hit the headlines regularly. What isn't as well reported, of course, is the number of cases when hypnosis

ANSWERS:

1. A soothing cerulean blue.
2. $5.
3. The Grinch that stole Christmas.
4. Holly.
5. Mango-Kiwi-Tropical Swirl.
6. *American Ronin*.

7. ". . . a core of uranium, or some damn thing."
8. He caught himself on fire.
9. Robert Patrick Modell.
10. F. Johnson.

YOUR SCORE _____

failed to turn up a single new detail—or the number of times that hypnotically obtained evidence *contradicted* known events and details. Inconsistencies raise questions and allow scriptwriters the scope to scare us with the unproven answers to our most pertinent questions.

Can Anyone Be Hypnotized?

The short answer seems to be, "Yes!"

While some 5 percent or so of the population have difficulty achieving deep levels of hypnotic trance, given a desire to do so, a trusted hypnotist, and comfortable surroundings, few people are *incapable* of being hypnotized. Included among that 4 to 5 percent are those with intelligence quotients of less than 60, whose attention-span difficulties make it impossible for them to judge the effects of hypnotic induction.

Conversely, about 10 percent of the population achieve deep trance levels quite easily, many without the aid of a hypnotist, and some, like those athletes "in the zone," completely spontaneously. Musicians and actors frequently exhibit the type of alert concentration involved in formal hypnosis, as do computer artists and video-game players.

The remainder of the population, statistically the largest group, falls somewhere between the extremes, and, as with a single individual, performance will vary considerably.

Is There a "Type" of Person Most Susceptible?

It used to be thought that the gullible, or even the slightly neurotic, were the best candidates for hypnosis, that those who could be hypnotized were, in fact, a little lighter between the ears than the general population. Not so.

In a series of studies stretching from the 1930s until the present, in as divergent settings as the lab and the Antarctic (considered an interesting example of suggestibility in the absence of sensory stimuli), scientists have discovered just enough to keep them scratching their heads. Gender, intelligence, mental health, and personality traits like introversion and extroversion have *absolutely no* apparent connection to hypnotic suggestibility.

A series of standardized tests, generally referred to as the Stanford Hypnotic Susceptibility Scale, measures how well a subject conforms to the "typical" behavior of a hypnotized subject, but not necessarily how "hypnotizable" an individual may be. Oddly enough, however, there are a few physical clues that may provide some correlation. In one test, a subject is asked to look as high as he can without moving his head. In effect, he is being asked to roll his eyes. The greater the area of sclera, that white portion of the eyeball, visible, the better potential subject. What does the ability to play a childish fright prank have to do with hypnotizability? No one knows, and significant correlations are tantalizingly slow to emerge.

Of the few suspected to date, the so-called "Fantasy Prone Personality" is perhaps the most legitimate model. Unfortunately, as with most things Hollywood attempts to portray, the Fantasy Prone Personality suffers from an exotic—but erroneous—image. Far from the sadly delusional people usually portrayed, FPPs are often extraordinary achievers with an incredible willingness to evaluate all the facts before forming conclusions, unusually acute memories (often eidetic), above-average sensory acuity, and an ability to manipulate mental images that is in itself a form of genius. The FPP isn't a victim of fantasy, but an incredibly competent *manipulator* of fantasy, capable of using mental imagery in the same fashion that an architect uses models.

Frank Lloyd Wright, one such FPP, could build cathedrals in his mind before ever putting pencil to paper to record the images he had created. Lou Gehrig, another FPP, frequently commented on his ability to "see the whole pitch through from the moment it left the pitcher's hand." Hitting the ball was simply a matter of putting the bat where he *knew* the ball would eventually be. Sculptors who "chip away everything that isn't whale" to reveal the whale they see in a block of stone are also likely to be Fantasy Prone Personalities.

The vivid descriptions Pusher created with his words, whether of soft winds incapable of hurting anyone or of wads of fat sticking in Detective Burst's arteries, are certainly the types of imagery likely to engage the attention of the FPP and, by extension, be useful in any attempts to sway the beliefs, emotions, or perceptions of the intended subject.

Am I in Control?

The extent of the hypnotist's control is, of course, the center of all Svengali-type plots, and "Pusher," like its predecessors, took the legitimate fears of hypnotic subjects way over the top—at least that's what we'd like to believe.

In fact, thanks to something called "trance logic," people can indeed be gently coerced into the oddest of acts. Trance logic presumes that, without a reason not to, most people will try to do as they're told. For example, most hypnotic subjects, regardless of their faith in their hypnotist, won't purposely hold their hand in a fire. If trance logic could convince the subject that the flame wasn't real, however, any number of fingers might be singed.

In some cases, trance logic isn't even necessary. In a study directed at the question of whether hypnotic subjects were dangers to themselves or others, Lloyd Rowland discovered that not only would some subjects voluntarily stick their hands into boxes they believed contained rattlesnakes, they would throw what they believed to be harsh acids in another's face!

Suddenly, the Pusher isn't as fictional as we'd like. . . .

Rationalizations about the level of trust these subjects had for their hypnotist might alleviate some alarm, but only if you believe in the good intentions of all "trusted" hypnotherapists.

If hypnosis could induce criminal acts, you'd expect to find court records of the results—and you do. In 1993, Roger Belton, a hypnotherapist, was found guilty of complicity in the rape of Caroline Bedford, the wife of one of his patients, despite the fact that Belton was more than sixty miles away at the time of the crime. With the aid of session tapes confiscated from Belton's office, a jury took eighteen minutes to decide that Wade Bedford, previously a loving and gentle husband, would never have assaulted his wife without Belton's intervention.

Such cases remain rare, fortunately for the young science that promises so much medical relief, and of those that are reported, most fall into a different category of crime altogether. Of those hypnosis-related cases that have come to light in modern times, about 90 percent involve sexual misconduct on the part of the hypnotist, a crime that occurs in proportionately equal numbers among medical doctors and psychiatrists.

Then What About Post-Hypnotic Suggestions?

Whenever Daisy Callahan is at home at 8:00 P.M., she finds herself washing her hands thoroughly for five minutes. She used to do it, on average, 112 times per day. Charles Lukowitz stopped smoking in 1983 and has never felt a nicotine craving. Gayle Trenton-Carter delivered both of her eight-pound babies without any medication, and with nothing more than a "little initial discomfort." Each of them is delighted with the results of his or her hypnotherapy. Each of them is a conundrum for hypnosis researchers.

Standing behind hypnotherapy's beneficial effects without fully understanding the mechanisms behind this benevolent tampering, is the sort of hypocrisy that leaves prospective patients, and audiences, just a tad leery.

eXtras:

Amid a veritable flood of O.J. Simpson jokes, *The X-Files* played it subtle: "So . . . he's a killer *and* a golfer."

X

Many fans have speculated that the character name "Modell" was yet another sports reference, this time to the highly unpopular owner of the Baltimore Ravens, once known as the Cleveland Browns.

Code Name: "TESO DOS BICHOS"

CASE SUMMARY:

One death in Ecuador, another in Boston, a protest letter to the State Department, an unusual artifact, and a fervent activist add up to a politically motivated murder for Scully and, not surprisingly, something more bizarre for Mulder. However, when Scully's suspect disappears while in her custody, Mulder's theories begin to seem almost plausible.

EYEWITNESS STATEMENT:

"This is more powerful than any *man*! This is a spirit you're dealing with—the spirit of the amaru. This is not something you can put in handcuffs!"

—Bilac

DEEP BACKGROUND:

Letting Sleeping Bones Lie

"Personally, if someone digs me up in a thousand years, I hope there's a curse on them, too."

—Agent Fox Mulder

At 2:00 A.M. on April 5, 1923, nineteen weeks after opening the tomb of King Tutankhamen, Lord Carnarvon died and a new style of horror tale was about to be born. In less than a week, a Berlin filmmaker/producer announced plans to begin shooting *The Pharaoh's Revenge*. Britain's very first horror film, *The Ghoul*, played off the Tutankhamen theme and featured Boris Karloff, who, only the year before, came to prominence in Hollywood's response to the imagery of sand dunes, pith helmets, and underground treasure troves, *The Mummy*. So popular would *The Mummy* prove to be that it was quickly revived in *The Mummy's Hand* and *The Mummy's Curse*. The genre must have been incredibly popular. Audiences sat through all three films and never once complained about the rather obvious fact that both sequels used extended footage from the original!

All the films that would follow, and *The X-Files'* episode "Teso Dos Bichos," featured mysterious deaths, cursed grave sites, and the intrusive archaeologists who presumed to disturb these ancient bones. The real-life string of deaths following the opening of King Tutankhamen's tomb was certainly bizarre enough to inspire several hundred hours of celluloid.

While the curse traditionally begins showing its effectiveness with the death of Lord Carnarvon, local legend takes the tale back to the day the tomb was opened. According to legend, the first death struck not a person, but codiscoverer Carter's pet canary! While Carter and Carnarvon were busy opening the grave site, a cobra, long associated with the Pharaohs, slid into the bird's cage and devoured it—a *very* bad omen.

Carnarvon's death from a fly bite, of all the ludicrous causes possible, merely confirmed for many Egyptians the tales of curses and occult deathwatches they'd been raised on.

Even skeptics began wondering as the death toll rose. Among victims:

George Jay Gould, millionaire American, visits Luxor and dies of unknown causes.

Woolf Joel, one of Carnarvon's best friends, visits Luxor by boat and is swept overboard by unknown means.

Sir Archibald Douglas Reid, a radiologist who'd just signed an agreement with the Department of Antiquities in Cairo to X-ray Tut's body, dies of unknown causes.

H.G. Evelyn White, professor, Leeds University, removes papyrus material from a Coptic monastery and commits suicide after reading it.

Georges Benedite, Director of the Louvre's Egyptian Department, and M. Marcel Cassanova, College de France, both excavators in the Valley of the Tombs, die of unknown causes.

Colonel Aubrey Herbert, Lord Carnarvon's half brother, and present for the opening of King Tut's sarcophagus, dies of "temporary insanity."

Evelyn Greely, after leaving the site and returning to her home in Chicago, killed her son and then herself.

M. Gardian Laffleur, a professor at McGill University and houseguest of Carter's, dies the day after his inspection of the tomb. Once again, the causes are unknown.

Arthur Mace, MoMA employee and Carter's coauthor, dies while working on a second volume of King Tut works.

Richard Bethell, Carter's personal secretary while working the Luxor sites, is found dead in a chair at the Mayfair Club. Cause of death, unknown.

Lord Westbury, father of Richard Bethell, commits suicide by jumping from the seventh floor of a building just off the Mall. When his

TRIVIA BUSTER 19

Easy Stuff: *Take a single point for each correct answer.*

1. What was dug up in the hills of Ecuador?
2. Where were the artifacts sent?
3. Mona's dog, who ate the cat, who ate the rat, who ate rat poison, was named?
4. What was found in Dr. Lewton's car engine, in all the toilets in the ladies' room, and inside Sugar?
5. What attacks Scully beneath the museum?

Tougher Trivia: *These are two-pointers all the way.*

6. What sort of car did Dr. Lewton drive?
7. What did Bilac call the South American hallucinogenic?
8. What exactly did Mulder and Scully find in the tree?
9. How did the rats get into the museum?
10. What was the official cause of death for Mona Wustner, Alonzo Bilac, Craig Horning, and Dr. Lewton?

body was being taken to a crematorium—he was terrified of being embalmed and buried like King Tut—the hearse runs astray and kills an eight-year-old child.

Edgar Steele, only fifty-seven years old, but Custodial Director of the Egyptological section of the British Museum, dies during routine surgery of "undetermined" causes.

Bringing the legend of the curse full circle, Lady Elizabeth Carnarvon, in a stroke of almost unbelievable serendipity, dies from, of all the ludicrous causes possible, a fly bite.

Even Scully might find such a string of odd occurrences and coincidences outside the percentages of random chance.

As an example of the "curse" form of horror story, "Teso Dos Bichos" isn't particularly remarkable—except it introduces an angle that would never have occurred to Carter or his contemporaries, namely, the cultural provenance of the artifacts and bones currently residing in museums thousands of miles from their country of origin. The same items that Carnarvon and Carter brought out of the "cursed" tomb, that are proudly displayed by such prestigious institutions as the British Museum and the Metropolitan Museum of Art, are the same objects that Egypt is now seeking to have returned.

It's estimated that a billion dollars a year pass through the hands of grave-looters and uptown art dealers alike; countries like Turkey, Mali, and Afghanistan often fail to see the distinction.

ANSWERS:

1. An urn containing the remains of a woman shaman, an amaru.
2. To the Boston Museum of Natural History.
3. Sugar.
4. Rats.
5. A cat.
6. A Jaguar.
7. Vine of the Soul. (Take a single point if you said Yagë.)
8. Four feet of human duodenum and a foot of ilium. (One point if you came up with "intestine.")
9. Through vents leading to the old steam-tunnel heating system.
10. Animal attack.

YOUR SCORE _____

In 1994, a New York University professor strolling down Madison Avenue was startled to see an artifact that he himself had excavated from a Turkish site propped up in the window of a ritzy art dealership. The dealer immediately denied any suggestion that the piece could have been stolen, despite the professor's eyewitness account of the statue's history. However, when the Federal Bureau of Investigation was notified, and Turkey's representatives began pressing hard, the gallery quickly and quietly removed the piece from the window and returned it to Turkish authorities.

Turkey's most publicized effort to reclaim its cultural heritage involved no other giant than the New York Metropolitan Museum of Art. After a six-year battle through the courts, a massive collection of artifacts made from several precious metals, the Lydian Hoard, was returned to Turkey—but with no fault recognized on the part of the museum. That may change next time around. It's already back in court, with Afghanistan this time, arguing over whether the top half of a significant statue should be reunited with the bottom half still residing in its original home.

Collectors, universities, and museums around the world are watching the outcome of these "cultural patrimony" cases closely. Not only because of the wealth of foreign artifacts filling North American and European display cases, but because the looting isn't just something that happens "over there." Current artifact tracing indicates that better than half the National Protected Areas in the United States have been looted. It seems the only restriction on who's suing whom for custody of what, is money. Litigation can cover several continents, involve reams of paperwork in a multitude of languages, and stretch out for years.

Considering the heel-dragging, teeth-grinding routine that usually accompanies a request to repatriate even those artifacts that everyone agrees are common and relatively insignificant, the Musée Jalahanan was pleasantly surprised to have one of its most desirable artifacts, a set of pre-Columbian urns, returned from Germany without any arguments whatsoever.

The museum's curators were less pleased when Dr. Pasharin, who managed to procure this piece so easily, died unexpectedly, as did his replacement. They were even more inconvenienced when Mr. Graham

Kent, their legal representative in the U.S., died the following week. They began to look suspiciously at their latest acquisition when two of their staff became ill within the week. Whether from superstition or a burgeoning sensitivity to the feelings of indigenous peoples, the Musée Jalahanan made no objection to the suggestion that the pieces, identified as funerary items, be reinterred in the sacred burial ground from which they'd been removed.

How very X-Filean.

eXtras:

"Killer kitties": How Gillian Anderson described this episode during a nationally televised interview.

X

Due to Gillian Anderson's allergy to cats, the puppet that attacked Dana Scully was made of rabbit fur, which had the unpleasant habit of flying off the puppet and sticking to Anderson's lipstick.

Code Name: "HELL MONEY"

CASE SUMMARY:

How to arrest a ghost? That's the dilemma Agent Mulder is contemplating as he and Agent Scully arrive in San Francisco's Chinatown to investigate a series of deaths featuring crematory ovens as the murder weapons. Finding an astonishing variety of organs missing from her autopsy subjects, Dana Scully is looking for a more "solid" suspect.

EYEWITNESS STATEMENT:

"I find it hard to argue with two thousand years of Chinese belief, the stuff my parents and grandparents believe in. But the truth is, I'm more haunted by the size of my mortgage payments."
—**Detective Glen Chao, SFPD**

DEEP BACKGROUND:

Playing God

The "average" North American, if such a thing exists, will never donate an organ, receive one, or even glance twice at the little slip attached to his driver's license. Though organ donation is undoubtedly one of the most successful procedures available to medicine, one that arguably costs the donor nothing, organ donors are hard to find—unless you live in China.

While crime is supposedly on the rise worldwide, a number of human rights groups, including the Red Cross, Al-haradan, and Amnesty International, raised their collective eyebrows when the amount of executions in mainland China rose nearly 50 percent in a single year—the same year Asians from dozens of countries discovered China was *the* place to be if you needed a nice, fresh kidney, or liver, or heart.

The Chinese citizen on the street is no more naive than his American or European counterpart, and the distinct division between the great masses and the select group forming the head table in any picture of a Communist Party meeting is a recognized reality. The lists of citizens awaiting the most common transplant organ, the kidney, is so long that one in ten thousand will be accommodated before he dies or becomes so ill as to be unsuitable as a transplant candidate. At the annual general meeting of high-ranking Communist Party officials in 1994, however, 23 percent of the men present had received a donor organ in the past seven years, and 9 percent had received two or more organs. And despite its own long waiting list, China has apparently found more "perfect matches" between Chinese organs and non-Chinese but wealthy foreigners than among its own Chinese population.

If current demand continues and the frightening figures can be ex-

TRIVIA BUSTER 20

Easy Stuff: *Take a single point for each correct answer.*

1. What card game was featured on the Guard's hand-held video game?
2. Where did Johnny Lo die?
3. Name one of the exotic medical items Chao described to Scully.
4. What does Scully find inside a cadaver's chest?
5. How did Hsin explain the bandage over his eye?

Tougher Trivia: *These are two-pointers all the way.*

6. How many people were incinerated in total?
7. For what company did Mr. Hsin work?
8. What festival did Detective Chao suggest might be involved in the murders?
9. What unusual substance did Scully find on the corpse and Mulder find on a floor?
10. Which Chinese character corresponds to "eye"?

trapolated, it seems China will have 2100 percent more executed prisoners with harvestable organs just five years from now.

The potential profit margin to China?

Somewhere in the very comfortable neighborhood of a billion American dollars. The relatively simple kidney transplant brings in US $45,000. A heart transplant is reported to have been conducted for a Hong Kong businessman at the "very reasonable" rate of only US $115,000. "Express delivery," for any patient requiring life-saving surgery in less than three months, can nearly double the price. Not bad for a "renewable" resource.

Needless to say, tracing the path of any given organ back to its original owner can be difficult. For a nation where "clerks" have been recognized professionals for several thousand years, China seems to have incredible difficulty hanging on to its paperwork and acknowledging the criminal tendencies in the regions surrounding its hospitals. Local policing agencies haven't requested more personnel to deal with the violent offenders who have, according to execution records, been picking hospital zones as their preferred residential areas. In fact, according to China's justice divisions, criminal activity is practically uniform across the country.

Hospitals, which buy whole corpses from nearby prisons, can't explain the apparent contradiction in arrest and execution rates, and are quick to claim their dealings are completely aboveboard. The fact that executions—traditionally carried out with a single shot to the base of the skull, which conveniently leaves the majority of organs in harvestable condition—increased sharply *only* in those prisons close to hospitals technologically capable of performing transplants has gone officially unnoticed. So, too, did an odd policy change at a prison near People's Hospital 12. For reasons that neither prison officials nor hospital administrators want to discuss, the prison elected that execution would be by a single gunshot to the heart instead of to the head. If People's Hospital 12 is noted for anything, it is the success rate of its cornea transplants. Coincidence? Only if the game is as rigged as the one featured in "Hell Money."

While the ability to harvest and transplant organs reliably is a recent innovation in China, China's official policies and laws are firmly entrenched. The sale of organs is officially prohibited on obvious grounds. However, in 1984, China legalized the harvesting of organs from executed prisoners if three supposedly stringent requirements had been met: if the prisoner's body hadn't been claimed by the family, if the prisoner consented to the organ removal, and if the prisoner's family had given its consent. The practicalities of the Chinese prison and legal systems, however, make such niceties meaningless.

In China, no prisoners can technically be executed without the approval of the Supreme People's Court, which means *no* prisoners can sign documents or consent forms required to allow donation or even the multitude of medical tests necessary to prepare for organ transplantation. And since Chinese executions are nothing if not prompt—executions are carried out immediately following the reading of the verdict—there's simply no time for the proper medical screenings to be done beforehand! Either the organs are harvested without consent, or the laws are simply being ignored in favor of convenience.

The provision for a family to claim a body is equally meaningless. According to a law in the same section of the Chinese judicial code, "the family of an executed prisoner has no legal right to the body." The cremated remains—prisoners are seldom allowed to waste space by being buried—provide no clue for relatives who suspect organ harvesting.

As "Hell Money" suggested, organ theft may not be confined to China. A mother in San Francisco's Chinatown was delighted to discover she was a match for a daughter desperately in need of an alterna-

ANSWERS:

1. Blackjack.
2. In a crematory oven.
3. Ginseng, turmeric, bear gallbladder, snake, shark fin, skullcap root, or Chinese angelica.
4. A frog.
5. An accident with a carpet tack.

6. Three in Seattle, three in Los Angeles, two in Boston, and four in San Francisco, totaling twelve.
7. Bay Area Carpeteers.
8. Festival of the Hungry Ghosts.
9. Sterile ice.
10. Wood.

YOUR SCORE _____

tive to dialysis. Mrs. Marjorie Hsin's first examination, however, dashed the hope she and her daughter had been cautiously nursing. The scar Mrs. Hsin had been told was the result of her appendectomy several years earlier looked suspiciously out of place to the attending surgeon. An ultrasound confirmed his suspicions. Mrs. Hsin's appendix was indeed gone—along with one of her kidneys. She wasn't alone. In the following eighteen months, twenty-three other patients, all having shared the same doctor, discovered missing organs.

In 1993, two organ-transplant specialists became suspicious of a young man and his "father." While they shared certain biological factors which made the younger man a perfect donor for the elder, a health questionnaire revealed some disturbing inconsistencies. Although the two men claimed to have lived together since the young man's birth, the younger "Chang" had no idea his father smoked a pack and a half of cigarettes per day. The father left the "Spouse's Name" section blank on one form, and gave an incorrect response on another. Calling in the police, who quietly investigated the two men, revealed they'd met exactly two months previously. The physician who'd introduced the two charged a mere US $15,000 for his unique "matchmaking" service, US $2,500 of which was to be given to the donor as a "gratuity." Perhaps more frightening than even the cold-blooded marketing of body parts and the pressure brought to bear on unwilling donors is the seeming inability to prosecute the violators. In the Chang case above, no charges related to the sale of human organs were ever made, and even pressing charges on the attempt to defraud the insurance company were difficult to prove.

It seems a short step indeed to the horror hinted at in "Hell Money."

eXtras:

California waiting times:

Golden State Transplant Services, Sacramento
Kidney: 268 days
Heart: 160.5 days

California Transplant Donor Network, San Francisco
Kidney: 720 days
Liver: Not available
Heart: Not available

UCSD Medical Center, San Diego
Kidney: 790 days
Liver: 52 days
Heart: 106 days

Regional OPA of Southern California, Los Angeles
Kidney: 810 days
Liver: 48 days
Heart: 192 days

Southern California Organ Procurement Organization,
    Los Angeles
Kidney: 719 days
Liver: 42 days
Heart: 212–380 days

National median waiting times:

Kidney: 602 days
Liver: 146 days
Heart: 218 days

X

The Hell Money that inspired the title of this episode is available in most sizable Chinese communities, as is Hell Gold, Hell Houses, Hell Cars, and even Hell Clothes, all designed to make the spirits of those in the otherworld a little more comfortable.

X-REFERENCE:

Take Me Out to the Ball Game . . . Any Game

X-Philes, noted for their ability to ferret out the most obscure references or catch the most subtle of on-screen clues, would have to have been wrapped in cotton wool and stored away in a box on some shelf not to have recognized the X-crew's preoccupation with all things sporting. While it was most noticeable during the first two seasons when the writing team of Morgan and Wong slid sports references into almost all their episodes, it remained a recognizable trademark of the program through the third season, and, with rumors that Morgan and Wong will contribute to *The X-Files* once again while between projects, it's likely to pop up repeatedly as we head into season four.

How many of these do you remember?

"Deep Throat": Colonel Buddahas, a Green Bay fan, easily recalling the Super Bowl of 1968, right down to details like Don Chandler's four field goals and the fact that it was Vince Lombardi's last game, but can't remember how to fly.

"Conduit": When Mulder needs some quickie information from Danny Bernstein, his buddy over in the Cryptology section, he promises him tickets to a Redskins game from a friend of a friend of a friend if Danny will just eyeball the binary sequences young Kevin has been copying from the TV.

"Ice": Dr. Denny Murphy isn't just a sports fan, he's a fanatic, listening to his own customized audiotape collection of his all-time favorite plays on his headphones. Must be an extensive collection, too; it goes at least as far back as the 1982 football playoffs.

"Eve": Deep Throat offers to take Mulder to a Warriors game, as he was "just in the neighborhood."

"Beyond the Sea": Even the bad guys take a break for a football game. Luther Lee Boggs strangled his family over Thanksgiving dinner, but paused to watch the fourth quarter of the Detroit–Green Bay game. Well, guess that explains why Thanksgiving is the single most active day for officers responding to domestic violence calls.

"Young at Heart": For Mulder, a peaceful afternoon watching high school kids play football in the rain can't be ordinary either. As he watches a former partner's kid play, the partner's murderer is leaving poetry in his car.

"E.B.E.": Mulder and Deep Throat bemoan their inability to catch a game together at Camden Yards, Mulder figuring that DT should have the "connections" to get great seats if circumstances didn't make it impossible for them to sit together in the stands.

"Tooms": What do stretchy mutants with a taste for liver watch on TV? Sports, of course! In addition to four hours of BaBa Booey, Tooms spent his first night out of custody taking in a Phillies game and an Orioles game.

"Little Green Men": In this version of Samantha's abduction, the young Fox Mulder is wearing a New York Knickerbockers jersey with "KING" and "30" emblazoned across it.

"Blood": As a kid, it seems Mulder shared the usual passion for sports common to young men, playing right field.

"Red Museum": How can you tell if your child has been inoculated with hybridized DNA? See if he gives up football. When Mulder and Scully investigate the disappearance of a young man, Gary Caines, one of the sheriff's key points of evidence for the boy's change of temperament is the fact he stopped wanting to play football.

"Irresistible": Perhaps the ultimate sports allusion in the X-Filean universe played on creator Chris Carter's name. In this episode, Mulder's plans to attend a Viking game are thwarted by the appearance of a necro-fetishist demanding his time and attention. As they consult with Agent Brock, the game plays on a desktop TV in the background. The footage aired features real-life Viking player Chris Carter making a first down and then a touchdown in a flying over-the-top maneuver.

While locked up in jail, Donny Pfaster's blockmate can't recall Mulder's name but easily comes up with: "She was Scully, like that baseball announcer."

"Die Hand Die Verletzt": Think football can save the unwary from demon worship? Well, maybe. Given a choice between ending the PTA with a prayer to the dark powers or watching the game, at least one of the teachers, Paul, would rather have watched the game! Too bad they didn't have more that week.

On or off the set, basketballs are bouncing.

Sports allusions even turn up in the credits for this episode. San Diego Chargers fans Morgan and Wong added something special to their credits in the week before the Super Bowl.

"Fresh Bones": Even if there's not a football field within miles of the scene of the action, you can still work in a football reference or two. Jack MacAlpin might have spent most of this episode just wandering about, but according to his wife, he believed in only three things: the Marines, his family, and football.

"Fearful Symmetry": After all Morgan and Wong's sports references, and their public support of the Chargers as Super Bowl contenders, it was only to be expected that, following its miserable defeat, the Chargers, as well as Morgan and Wong, would come under gentle fire. Listen to the conversation between the construction workers. Wonder how often the dynamic writing team heard *that* over the weeks following their team's defeat!

"Pusher": In episodes like "Pusher," the Bad Guy of the Week could have led the agents on any wild-goose chase he chose. He chose a driving range.

Even the set decorators get in on the act with sports equipment popping up everywhere. In season one, Lauren Kyte ("Shadows") just happens to keep a baseball bat in the closet. Mulder spends three years working off those nervous moments while awaiting an answer to his illuminated Xs by slamming a basketball against his apartment floor. Perhaps we'll eventually see him investigating the people in the apartment below. After all, how many tenants would put up with that racket and not complain? The same basketball turns up in other locations as well, including the bedroom of a Navajo teenager where the ball is bounced around by an earthquake instead of Mulder.

With a lead character named after Vin Scully, the voice of the Dodgers, a creator who used to edit *Surfing* magazine, a male lead who hit university on a sports scholarship, and writers who actually believed the Chargers had a chance, was there ever a possibility that

Mulder would choose chess as his sport of choice? Or that Scully *wouldn't* know there was no football on Thursday night? Not really.

eXtras:

X-Philes may soon have good cause to wish sports and *The X-Files* a little farther apart. With the proposed move to Sunday nights, and the potential for conflicts with Fox's football coverage, X-Philes will be riding those remote controls a little more attentively than in the past.

Code Name:
"JOSE CHUNG'S *FROM OUTER SPACE*"

CASE SUMMARY:

When Scully attempts to re-create the events surrounding an alien abduction for docu-novel writer Jose Chung, he discovers that the truth, even for FBI agents, is both elusive and illusionary. Despite being given this second chance to record the "facts," Scully herself has difficulty reconciling the multiple viewpoints that make up the case's primary evidence.

EYEWITNESS STATEMENT:

"Your scientists have yet to discover how neural networks create self-consciousness, let alone how the human brain processes two-dimensional retinal images into the three-dimensional phenomenon known as *perception*! Yet *you* somehow brazenly declare 'Seeing is believing'?"

—Man In Black One

DEEP BACKGROUND:

Good-bye and Thanks for All the Fish

When "Jose Chung's *From Outer Space*" first aired, Darin Morgan, the comic genius who also penned "Humbug" and "War of the Coprophages," was talking about "burnout" and "a change of scene." This episode, with its allusion-a-minute pacing, certainly gave every sign of being a swan song. It was as if Morgan and crew were intent on cramming every allusion and in-joke they could into the forty-seven minutes of screen time. How many did you catch?

Alien Autopsy: As in the episodes "Nisei" and "731," this is a poke at the Fox network, which aired the infamous "Alien Autopsy: Fact or Fiction" not once but *three* times.

BLEEP!: Named for Director Kim Manners, Detective Manners shares another characteristic with his namesake, a tendency to curse volubly.

Book Cover: A quick glance at the covers of Jose Chung's *From Outer Space* and Whitley Streiber's tale of alien abduction *Communion* will explain the design of the former.

Cigarette-Smoking Alien: Along with the obvious association with The Cigarette-Smoking Man, the tobacco industry is swiftly becoming known for one of the broader true-life conspiracies in modern times. Information leaking out strongly suggests that not only were the tobacco companies aware of the health hazards of cigarettes

TRIVIA BUSTER 21

Easy Stuff: *Take a single point for each correct answer.*

1. What oddity was noticed in connection with Chrissy's clothes after she was found?
2. It's not an alien, but something in Chrissy's room certainly looked like one. What?
3. What mantra did the caged gray alien keep muttering?
4. According to MIBs, what planet is most often confused with a UFO?
5. What made the Gen-Xer Blaine think Scully was in reality one of the Men In Black?

Tougher Trivia: *These are two-pointers all the way.*

6. From what affliction did Mulder believed Chrissy suffered?
7. Who did Jose Chung describe as having "colorful phraseology"?
8. Which political party did Roky Crikenson prefer?
9. What was unusual about Roky's "manifesto"?
10. Scully discovered a medical oddity when she performed the postmortem on the "alien." What?

all along, but they purposefully "spiked" their products to ensure higher levels of addiction.

Jose Chung: Carl Gustav Jung, the psychologist, wrote a monograph entitled "Flying Saucers: A Modern Myth of Things Seen in the Skies."

Klass County: Philip Klass authored *UFOs: The Public Deceived* and *UFOs Explained*, which postulate that UFO sightings are the result of a perfectly natural phenomenon like light refracting through clouds or ball lightning. Klass also moderates CSICOP's UFO subcommittee. He penned the line: "No single object has been misinterpreted as a 'flying saucer' more often than the planet Venus."

Lord Kinbote: From the Vladimir Nabokov novel about arbitrary realities, *Pale Fire*, Lord David Kinbote, like Jose Chung, is the ultimate in unreliable narrators.

Mashed Potatoes: Alludes to that classic, *Close Encounters of the Third Kind*. The character played by Richard Dreyfuss, Roy Neary, a linesman like this episode's Roky, sculpts a plate of mashed spuds into the Devil's Tower before undertaking a larger model that eventually occupies his whole living room.

MIB 1: This MIB, portrayed by WWF wrestler Jesse "the Body" Ventura, is the one who drops poor Gen-Xer Blaine with a probably patented "back breaker" move.

MIB 2: Another in this season's list of "Dig David" gags following his surprising loss on Celebrity *Jeopardy*, Alex Trebek's appearance was a riot, but Trebek wasn't the first choice for the role. Who else did they have in mind? The Original Man In Black—Johnny Cash.

ANSWERS:

1. She was wearing them inside out and backward.
2. A stuffed cat at the foot of her bed.
3. "This is not happening."
4. Venus.
5. Her hair was too red.
6. Postabduction syndrome.
7. Detective Manners.
8. The Republicans.
9. It was written in screenplay format.
10. A zipper.

YOUR SCORE _____

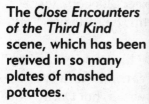

The *Close Encounters of the Third Kind* scene, which has been revived in so many plates of mashed potatoes.

Military/Industrial/Entertainment Complexes: Among the many in existence, take RCA/NBC as an example. Owned by parent company GE, they bring bombs "to life" as well as their light bulbs and entertainment products. The reference begins with the farewell speech of President Eisenhower, who warned the American people and their government that "military-industrial complexes" like Boeing were becoming all-too-powerful lobbyists in D.C.

MKULTRA: MKULTRA and MKDELTA supposedly existed in order to plant unknowing spies in enemy territory. The idea was to implant the order to spy and report to their CIA control—but never know they'd done so until a second round of hypnosis and other mind-control techniques "reintroduced" the spies to the hidden portion of their lives.

Ovaltine Diner: The Ovaltine Diner is a real Vancouver landmark, located at 251 East Hastings.

Red Aliens: The late arrival to the alien abduction bore a striking resemblance to one of monster-maker-extraordinaire Ray Harryhausen's creations for *Twenty Million Miles to Earth*. The monster was a Vesuvian. "All you saw was Venus."

Reynard Mandrake: The word *reynard* is French for "fox."

Roky's Bucket: The underside of the lineman's bucket, shot against the night sky, mimics the Imperial Star Cruisers from *Star Wars*.

Sgt. Hynek: A direct reference to none other than J. Allen Hynek, a prominent figure in both astronomy and UFO circles. Among his many activities is a cameo in *Close Encounters of the Third Kind*— after working as a creative consultant for the film. As an investigator, he coauthored a number of books, including one with Jacques Vallee, and was a leading member of the Project Bluebook team.

Sign-off: The theme music played at the end of this episode was "off" by a single note.

***Space: Above and Beyond* Sweatshirt:** Catch Blaine's sweatshirt? Makes sense when you recall that Glen Morgan, an executive producer for *Space*, is not only a former X-Filean writer, but Darin Morgan's equally twisted older brother. While appearing on *Space*, Duchovny portrayed AL, an artificially intelligent "mandroid."

Spheres and Obelisks: Check out the shelving in Jose Chung's office. If you see the sphere and obelisk, think back to "Aubrey" as well as *2001: A Space Odyssey*.

Sweet Potato Pie: A reference to another fictional FBI agent, Dale Cooper of *Twin Peaks*. Cooper, who actually preferred cherry pie, was renowned for the bite-question-bite-question-bite routine aped by Duchovny's character in this episode. David Duchovny himself portrayed the transvestite character Dennis/Denise on the same program.

U.S. Pilots Richard Vallee and Jacques Shaeffer: Switch the names around and you come up with Jacques Vallee, who investigated the Philadelphia Experiment and wrote about it as well as about UFOs and possible disinformation schemes involving them; and Schaeffer, whose UFO pictures appeared in Klass's *UFOs Explained*.

". . . a little too red . . ." Actress Gillian Anderson, a blond until being cast as Dana Scully, dyed her hair for the role.

"His face was so blank and expressionless." The popular press has, from time to time, commented on Duchovny's tendency to intensity instead of the overblown acting so common on episodic television. Morgan makes a similar statement in "Humbug" when another character compares him to a *GQ* layout.

"This isn't happening . . .": Shades of *Aliens* where Bill Paxton's character, Hudson, spends the entire film muttering the same phrase to himself.

Of course, on a broader scale, Darin Morgan once again dipped into the best of film history. Films like Kurosawa's *Rashomon* also explore the multiplexity of perception, while *The Manchurian Candidate*, referenced in this episode as "The Caligarian Candidate," takes that a step farther, graphically illustrating the warped perceptions of a brainwashed soldier. The other half of that reference, *The Cabinet of Dr. Caligari*, revives the story of a hypnotic magician and the victims who followed his most bizarre orders, or maybe the story of a deranged psychiatrist, or maybe the deranged patients, or maybe . . . Well, no one's quite sure *what* it's about, are they?

Just as Darin Morgan played heavily into *The X-Files'* tendency for self-referencing, a number of events and appearances in "Jose Chung's *From Outer Space*" were direct references back to Morgan himself. The Tarot Reader from his earlier episode "Clyde Bruckman's Final Repose," also the Museum Curator from "Humbug," reappears as a hypnotist in this episode. The Stupendous Yappi, also from "Clyde Bruckman's Final Repose," reprised the role here, with equal panache. The "girlie scream" postulated in "War of the Coprophages" is finally delivered here. Add in the subtitle of "Alien Autopsy: Truth or Humbug," a reference to Morgan's first script, "Humbug," and it comes full circle.

eXtras:

The X-Files seems to delight in sending its fans scurrying for their dictionaries.

Confabulation: (n) chat of a spurious nature, the precursor to rumor.

X

The X-Files is becoming well known for its inclusion of alternative music, so when a character named Roky Crikenson turns up, it's a small leap to Roky Erickson, who sang lead for Thirteenth Floor Elevators while investigating the music resulting from combining studio time and mind-altering drugs. The name of his next group, Roky Erickson & The Aliens, may reflect the singer's sporadic belief that he himself is a Martian.

Code Name: "AVATAR"

CASE SUMMARY:

Assistant Director Walter Skinner discovers how quickly the tables can turn when he wakes up with a dead prostitute in his bed and it's Scully and Mulder who must try to prove *his* innocence to both the police and the Office of Professional Conduct. Skinner's natural reticence, conflicting evidence, and an incredibly inconvenient bout of amnesia conspire to make the job more difficult, but it's Cigarette-Smoking Man's shadowy presence that may prove the most ominous.

Mitch Pillegi as A. D. Skinner, a role he models after his own father

EYEWITNESS STATEMENT:

"In the Middle Ages, a visitation like the one Skinner described would have been attributed to a succubus, a spirit that visits men in the night, usually in the form of an old woman."

—Special Agent Fox Mulder

The Taxonomy of Monsters

In *The X-Files'* universe, theories abound. Even fanatical X-Philes have lost track of the number of times Scully's eyes have rolled in response to Mulder's latest notion—only to discover the situation really isn't as rational as she'd thought. In rare episodes like "Revelations," it's Mulder's own perverse skepticism that gives way to Scully's brand of belief. Rarely, however, do we get to see them *both* be wrong!

Perhaps because of Skinner's reticence to fork over the juicy details of his otherworldly encounters, or because Mulder—fresh from contact with his "video collection"—was more attuned to the sexual undertone of the episodes, he came up with an intriguing but totally misplaced theory. It has often been suggested that UFOs are the North American answer to our lack of European-style haunted castles, our own bit of folklore. That may or may not be true, but North America is definitely rife with bits and pieces of the Old Country's tales.

The succubus is a well-traveled monster, popular in Egyptian, East Indian, and Asian mythoi, as well as in Europe, where it's enjoyed

TRIVIA BUSTER 22

Easy Stuff: *Take a single point for each correct answer.*

1. What was the obvious cause of death for Carina Sayles?
2. What color was Sharon Skinner's raincoat?
3. Where was Agent Bonnecaze's home office?
4. What "look-alike" Scotch brand does Skinner drink?
5. What piece of evidence did Mulder deliver to Agent Pendrell for analysis?

Tougher Trivia: *These are two-pointers all the way.*

6. How long have Walter and Sharon Skinner been married?
7. What's Scully's explanation for Skinner's "nightmares"?
8. What's written inside Walter Skinner's wedding band?
9. What did Scully think might cause the glow around the murdered hooker's mouth?
10. What does the "S" in Walter S. Skinner stand for?

semiofficial status for centuries. In Wallasey alone, some 130 men reported being assaulted by succubi in a single court season, which is less than eight months long. In Scotland, a Hector Boece made repeated complaints to his parish priest and even his bishop about a "she-demon" who "so sapped him of his manliness as to make him useless to his wife." His priest's suggestion—that he try fasting, bathing in a nearby stream known for its icy headwaters, and long bouts of prayer—did nothing to relieve him of the mysterious woman's attentions. In fact, Boece's moans and cries, the audible results of his visitor's ministrations, soon irritated his neighbors to the point of making formal complaints.

Boece's bishop, apparently at the urging of Boece's wife, took a more active role in the "affair." He moved in, claimed the most comfortable chair in the home, and sat watch over Hector Boece. He didn't have long to wait. Shaken, he emerged the following morning to write, "Truly, the man is possessed by the creature, knowing nothing from the moment of her arrival until, spent, he's tossed back to the shores of consciousness. No attempts to awaken him were successful, nor did the creature cringe from my Holy abjuration to leave the house."

Treating the incident as a form of possession, Bishop Ainan Prescote sent the man's wife to stay with relatives, salted the foundations of the home, and, armed with the tools of his trade, took up residence once again. A local constable, Ian Bell, arrived on the second day to investigate the screams shattering Boece's neighbors' sleep. He emerged after less than a quarter of an hour. Once past the Boeces' gate, he refused to discuss anything he'd seen, merely telling nearby residents to "pass this place without so much as a glance towards

---

ANSWERS:

1. A broken neck.
2. Red.
3. Norfolk.
4. J&P, a look-alike for J&B.
5. The air bag from Skinner's car.
6. Seventeen years.
7. REM-sleep behavior disorder.
8. "LOVE FOREVER SHARON."
9. A fungal growth of some sort.
10. Sergei.

YOUR SCORE _____

it until the good Bishop himself tells us that all's well within those walls."

The "good bishop" wasn't making any such claim that night, or for the next eleven nights either.

When Hector Boece's wife was finally allowed to come home, and a gaunt bishop staggered out to the nearest kirk, Hector Boece had "lost three stone and looked as content as e'er a man looked." Mrs. Boece apparently settled back in with her man, satisfied that his bizarre mistress wasn't wandering through her walls or making not-so-secret assignations with her husband.

The tale, in one form or another, repeats itself throughout European folklore. A Sicilian man, thinking he was saving a beautiful woman from drowning, inadvertently took his succubus home with him. He didn't realize his mistake until she'd taken advantage of his "hospitality" long enough to bear a child, which she then stole before disappearing. In Poland, the succubus became a legal reality when one stood before a judge, was tried, and then was convicted of demonism. The priest had reported a beautiful woman who simply materialized in the village of Jaklow, where she seduced dozens of the village's most eligible men, several of whom died in her bed. Although she was sentenced to death by burning, the woman disappeared as mysteriously as she'd arrived. On the morning of her execution, her cell was found locked but empty. In Axapta, Greece, the local populace made no attempt to destroy their beautiful succubus. She was their secret weapon, the one they turned on the leaders of invading city-states. Axapta remained independent until, tired of her virtual captivity, the beautiful woman simply walked through the wall of a house and failed to reappear on the far side.

Unfortunately, the key elements in all these tales work against Mulder's theory that Skinner was being visited by one of the beautiful temptresses. While some evil demons are traditionally described as Old Hags or Old Women, the succubi aren't. On the contrary, their central similarity has always been their incredible beauty. Their sexual favors didn't take holidays as long as the one between the Vietnam conflict and the present day either. Having picked her man, or men, the succubus is diverted only by her own precocious whims or the victim's death. Her interests are strictly sexual, seldom helpful in any way, and never involve the possession of other women. All in all, while interesting, this appears to be a case of Mulder applying the wrong folktale.

A much more likely candidate, both in appearance and in purpose, is Ireland's banshee. Like the succubus, the banshee is invariably female; in fact, the word "banshee" is loosely translated as "female fairy." Also like the succubus, the banshee is a single-minded creature. It picks an individual, and often his entire family, then spends the rest of its existence following their activities. Unlike the succubi, however, the banshees appear as women of all ages, some young and beautiful, almost childlike, others as twisted old crones. Their temperaments vary as much as their appearance, some delighting in the misery of their quarry, others acting as indifferent harbingers of death, others, as in the "Avatar" episode, taking on the role of protector.

One such protector, who is said to have attended the O'Reardons since 1634, is eerily reminiscent of Skinner's Woman in Red. Padraic O'Reardon, of Chicago, Illinois, was among the many young men who, with serious reservations, stepped off a troop carrier in Vietnam. Though long removed from the family home in Ireland, Padraic's family remained staunch believers in the old legends, and Padraic sincerely hoped the elusive spirit of the O'Reardons' banshee would remain as watchful as ever.

Two weeks later, he began to think maybe she had indeed found her way halfway around the world to a patch of jungle where Padraic O'Reardon and eleven other young men were hunched. Amid the drip of midday rain, Padraic began to think he was hearing things. A vague humming, irritating at a level just below the audible, set his teeth on edge. A check of the radio gear showed nothing odd there, nor did the sound appear to come from any of the other reasonable places he could think of. The hum grew louder as the day progressed and they approached the top of a ridge that was supposed to be under friendly control. By early evening, Padraic thought he was one of those people who simply couldn't take the oppressive, claustrophobic environment of the jungle. He thought he was hearing a voice singing just behind his ear: "Go back."

Anticipating a nasty tour of duty, if not a stay in a psychiatric hospital, as his inevitable fate, Padraic O'Reardon continued humping through the thick vegetation.

"Stop, Padraic. Stop."

Shaking his head, he turned and saw an old woman, not ugly, but certainly tortured-looking, staring back at him. Almost as soon as he caught sight of her, she screamed and faded into the curtains of rain.

Bullets whizzed past him, shredding the tree beside him. And one raked across his shoulder, embedding itself somewhere below his collarbone. Two men died as the group tried to backtrack, at night, through territory which had turned hostile without anyone bothering to notify them. O'Reardon was still on his feet, and remembers little of the trip back down the hillside—little beyond the glimpses of a woman whom he followed most of the night.

It might be interesting to discover if the character of Skinner has Irish roots. For the only thing that prevents his "visitor" from being termed a banshee is the fact that the banshees apparently take little interest in those not first from the Emerald Isle.

eXtras:

Seems Agent Pendrell has captured the hearts of the X-crew as well as of the audience. The part Brendan Beiser played in "Avatar" was originally cast for a new character named Dr. Rick Newton.

Code Name: "QUAGMIRE"

CASE SUMMARY:

Giving up a well-deserved weekend off to help Mulder investigate a series of Missing Persons Reports seems like a legitimate, if routine, enterprise to Scully—until she discovers his prime suspect is an American version of the Loch Ness monster! However, even Scully is willing to admit something unusual is afoot when bits and pieces of a half-dozen bodies begin "surfacing" around Heuvelmans Lake.

EYEWITNESS STATEMENT:

"Something [gasp] . . . something brushed up against me out there! Something . . . [gasp] big. Close the lake! Close it down! I want you to call the state police! And the Wildlife, Fish, and Game! You tell 'em we got an *emergency* situation!"

—**Sheriff Lance Heads**

DEEP BACKGROUND:

Here Be Monsters

Whether it's Nessie or any of her other scattered kin, and whether they exist or are, as Scully would say, an expression of our universal fear of the unknown, mysterious denizens of the deep remain one of the most widespread and enduring figures of our collective folklore.

While the most skeptical quickly point to the tourism value of such creatures, and to the individual profits possible for those who produce convincing evidence of their personal encounters, as the sole reasons for modern-day sightings, the more generous of spirit see no reason why today's generation would be more anxious to claim a watery close encounter than those living before the age of television specials and copyright.

There have, of course, also been hoaxes to confuse the issue. Perhaps the most famous of the lake monsters, Nessie, is known to have at least seven long-standing hoaxes associated with it. Of all the pictures purporting to be Nessie, one, taken by Colonel (Dr.) Robert Wilson in 1934, is known to have been reproduced over 6,000 times in various books, articles, and documentaries. Its relative clarity and mysterious lighting made it a popular smash for decades, and if you've seen only one of the many Nessie photos, you've likely seen the Wilson picture.

It's a fraud.

So, too, are photos by Frank Searle, Anthony Toreth, Mavis Bull, Tony Shiels, Mark Wharem, Wyatt Carnegie, and Carl Chorvinsky. While some of these images—like Mark Wharem's effort, which featured the top half of a commercial Godzilla costume—failed even the

TRIVIA BUSTER 23

Easy Stuff: *Take a single point for each correct answer.*

1. What was Scully's dog's name?
2. What was the common name for The Southern Serpent of Heuvelmans Lake?
3. What was written on Ted Bertram's cap?
4. The loss of what piece of equipment brought Dr. Bailey back to Striker's Cove and his death?
5. What did Mulder think he might be seeing amid Ansel Bray's collection of poorly focused photographs?

Tougher Trivia: *These are two-pointers all the way.*

6. For whom did Dr. Bailey work?
7. What unusual creature was pulled from a Massachusetts lake?
8. Which aquatic dinosaur did Mulder think might fit the description of "monsters" like Nessie and Ogopogo?
9. When was the supposed monster's scale found?
10. What song is Ansel Bray singing just before he meets the mysterious lake dweller?

The next Big Blue?

most casual inspection, others remained convincing until more modern techniques could assess lighting, angles of refraction and reflection, hydrodynamics, and film tampering.

Scratching seven names off the list of reputable Nessie sighters, however, didn't account for all the photographic evidence, and a core body of work remains as even more analytic techniques are applied to it.

Film, composed of perhaps thousands of individual frames which make the simpler forms of image tampering too difficult and time-consuming for even the determined hoaxer, is generally seen as the most reliable record. The special effects tackled by big movie studios aren't done at smaller studios *because* of their expense and complex

ANSWERS:

1. Queequag.
2. Big Blue.
3. "SHOW US YOUR BOBBERS."
4. A beeper.
5. The tooth of a lake monster.

6. The U.S. Forestry Service.
7. A bull shark.
8. A pleiosaur.
9. February 20, 1965.
10. "True Colors."

YOUR SCORE _____

technology. The same obstacles ensure that Joe Average with a portable movie camera or camcorder is pretty much out of the business of faking monsters. With that in mind, then, it's interesting to note that the images of Nessie that are considered most reliable are indeed on film!

Tim Dinsdale's footage, on simple 16-mm film, has been analyzed by some of the best, including the British RAF's Joint Aerial Reconnaissance Intelligence Centre, biologists ranging in specialties from biophysics to paleontology, and scores of hydrophysicists, film technicians, and special-effects designers. While none of these people seem quite sure what they're looking at, the film and the images on it are genuine. Their consensus: Whatever "it" may turn out to be, "it" extended some five feet above the water, was at least sixteen feet long, moved at speed, couldn't have been a boat, and, to all appearances, "was a living, an animate, object."

Hoaxers undoubtedly exist. So, too, do sincere individuals as anxious to identify the creatures they believe they've glimpsed as the skeptics themselves. And skeptics aren't immune to home-grown folklore of their own making either. When Douglas Quaid declared during the documentary *The Search for Dragons* that "all such sightings are best considered as innovative tourism marketing that traces its roots to the success of a Scottish village in luring the gullible to its shores," Nessie fans nearly fell off their chairs. Such claims sound good to some skeptics, and certainly cast doubt on the motives of those claiming sightings in other lakes, but the belief that Nessie "inspired" all the lake-monster tales is utter rubbish.

As skeptics like Ronald Binns rightly point out, Nessie isn't the ancient monster proponents sometimes present. In fact, the earliest sightings seem to stem from the early 1930s, making Nessie one of the *youngest* of the monsters reportedly living in some 250-plus lakes worldwide.

Lake Okanagan's Ogopogo, which, globally speaking, is a mere hop-skip-and-a-splash from *The X-Files'* shooting locations in Vancouver, was a well-established legend long before Nessie surfaced half a world away. In fact, considering the time interval involved—at least *500* years—and the varying size descriptions, Lake Okanagan is sometimes suspected of playing host to a small population of lake monsters.

Helping that notion along is the unusual nature of the sightings. On September 16, 1926, Okanagan Mission Beach was packed with late-season holiday-goers and thirty cars lined the roadside when Ogopogo surfaced. Whether as a result of the lighting or because Ogopogo prefers to "pod," many of the witnesses reported seeing a second figure, smaller, alongside the first. Multiple-observer sightings, while not proof of authenticity, certainly add credence to local verbal history. A series of multiple-observer sightings, still not proof but enough to bring serious scientists to the site, continue to this day.

Of course, long before H.F. Beattie came up with the ditty that named Ogopogo in 1924, British Columbia's First Nations Peoples knew the creature, or creatures, as N'ha-a-tik, Chinook for "Great-Beast-on-the-Lake," or Na-ha-ha-tik, Salish for "Snake-in-the-Lake."

Roy P. Mackal, one of the many cryptozoologists who have turned their attention to the remarkably consistent descriptions of Ogopogo, has postulated a theory a step removed from the one Mulder embraced—that lake monsters were pleiosaurs. He believes the sightings at Lake Okanagan accurately describe a primitive species of whale, *Basilosaurus cetoides*. For the First Nations Peoples who've lived with it for generations, taxonomic names are irrelevant—geography is the key.

Just as Mulder suspected Big Blue spent some portion of its day hidden in the woods around Striker's Cove, the Salish believe Na-ha-ha-tik includes a small island, Rattlesnake, in its territory. Aside from the unusual quantity of fish and small animal bones scattered around its shoreline, unwary fishing parties foolish enough to overnight there would occasionally awaken to discover themselves short a person. In 1914, the half-decayed body of an unknown animal was found on the beach there. Weighing in excess of 400 pounds, it had flippers and a tail, but the anterior portion suffered so badly from predation and decay that it was impossible to re-create the entire creature. The early explanation, that it was a manatee, is just as bizarre as the original Ogopogo theory.

Falling somewhere between Ogopogo's longevity and Nessie's relative youth are hundreds of other legendary creatures. Some, like the Chesapeake Bay's Chessie, South Bay's Bessie, and Lake Tahoe's Tessie, seem to vary considerably from sighting to sighting. Others, like the monsters inhabiting various lakes in Scandinavia, vary only in size.

Occasionally, the "truth" about these monsters startles even "believers." The X-Filean tale of the bull shark dragged out of a New England lake proves difficult to track down, and may be apocryphal, but other equally bizarre things have certainly been pulled up from their adopted homes. The giant squid, once passed off as the legendary kraken of Greek epic poetry, is a slimy reality today. Coelacanths, an ancient species of fish thought to be extinct for over seventy million years, resurfaced in fishermen's nets this century. (As they tended to explode on being brought to the surface, they, too, were often passed off as some other, more likely, species.) Fishermen off the coast of Japan reeled in a carcass weighing in excess of a ton that, even after a lifetime of experience with local species of fish, sharks, and whales, they couldn't identify. A conger eel, probably released when it became too large to qualify as a comfortable house pet, flourished in its new home and grew to an incredible *thirty-two* feet before frightening the daylights out of a diver and subsequently being captured.

If reality is so absurd, why not the long-necked, if nearly prehistoric, whale called a zeuglodon? Or other eels? Or . . . something altogether unknown?

If there is a real consistency to these stories, it may be the absolute conviction sighters have in the veracity of their encounters. Swedish Fisheries Officer Ragnar Bjvrks, who figured he'd seen everything there was to be seen in Lake Storsjvn, treated the lake's monster, Storsjvodjuret, as an amusing local myth. At least he did until the 350-year-old myth swam under his boat while he was randomly checking the permits of those fishing on the lake. Startled, Bjvrks took a swipe at it with his oar. He was even more startled when it swiped back—and tossed his boat ten feet into the air! Things like that tend to make even devout skeptics into believers.

eXtras:

This episode's Heuvelmans Lake was a nod to one of the most noted of water monster researchers, Bernard Heuvelmans, who wrote *In the Wake of the Sea Serpents*.

X

The *Patricia Rae*, the boat that sank in Heuvelmans Lake along with the agents' $500 deposit, was named in honor of writer Kim Newton's mother. Wonder what Freud would have made of that.

X

Scully tells us that Queequag was another *Moby Dick* character, but she neglects to mention that the harpoonist and her pooch share a more relevant trait—they both ate humans!

X

And more of the Name Game: The photographer's name in "Quagmire" was Ansel, an uncommon name, but best known for belonging to famed nature photographer Ansel Adams.

X

If the kids in this episode looked familiar, it's likely because they were pursuing a similar investigation into psychedelic substances in an attic in "War of the Coprophages."

Code Name: "WET WIRED"

CASE SUMMARY:

Scully's involvement in their latest case inches past the line of duty when, after an intensive stint as a couch potato, she "catches" the same violent paranoia afflicting their suspects, then disappears. With his partner reduced to just another suspect, Mulder's duties and his loyalties work against one another and the truth looks likely to be lost in the shuffle.

X—just X

EYEWITNESS STATEMENT:

"There's something nonstandard here, in the vertical blanking interval. Information that's being *added* into the spaces *between* the still pictures."

—**Bourse**, Editor, *The Lone Gunman*

DEEP BACKGROUND:

Something Lurking in Your Entertainment?

EAT POPCORN
EAT POPCORN
EAT POPCORN

Hardly a seditious or dangerous idea, but "Eat Popcorn," when slipped between the frames of films playing in theaters across North America, was perhaps the first time average Americans *knew* they'd been the victims of covert manipulation.

It was one thing for car companies to design bumpers, fenders, or hood ornaments to be "vaguely but satisfyingly sexual," and quite another to attempt imprinting specific messages—especially during an activity where the public felt themselves relatively free from the usual barrage of attempts to persuade them to do something, buy something, or believe something.

Traditional advertisements are expected to contain any number of techniques designed to separate consumers from their cash. Some of the techniques dubbed subliminal seem anything but to the modern, enlightened buyer. Draping a scantily clad woman over the hood of a car was once considered a subtle way of equating cars with power and sex. Today, it's not only obvious, but, in many circles, a distinct turnoff. Replacing the scantily clad woman with a scantily clad man, to appeal to the growing number of female buyers, didn't fly either.

While subliminal messages and images technically include anything that could induce a particular emotion, idea, or action by appealing to the sub- or unconscious parts of our minds, there are recognized categories of subliminals, some more publicly acceptable than others.

Advertisers and consumers acknowledge the game being played out between them as sellers use a broad spectrum of inducements to ensure their product is seen as the most attractive option. Famous faces, snazzy packaging, and bonus items describe the "Cracker Jack and Wheaties" approach to subliminal messages. Buyers recognize these maneuvers as ploys to sell products. Even the most naive of children realize that eating Wheaties isn't going to turn them into Wayne

Gretsky, but the fantasy is fun, and if we choose to pay for that as well as the cereal, that's up to the consumer.

Then there are the products *designed* to appeal to the unconscious parts of our minds. For a mere $14.95, anyone can pick up a forty-five-minute tape, audio or video, featuring the sounds of water splashing over rocks, waves rippling against the shore, or wind whispering through pines. Videos add images of dazzling sunsets over tropical beaches, a faux fish tank, hummingbirds in flight. And either one will get you subliminal voices suggesting, "Relaxation is a positive method of handling stress."

Heftier price tags deliver whole courses addressing a variety of self-improvement projects, everything from overcoming the nicotine habit to learning foreign languages to improving the ability to speak in public. By spending $1 billion each year on these self-directed forays into subliminals, the public clearly endorses them.

It's those subliminal messages that don't come as nicely labeled as a low-fat taco, for example, or that aren't as obvious as the traditional appeals to our need for sex, power, or luxury, that give people the heebie-jeebies.

TRIVIA BUSTER 24

Easy Stuff: *Take a single point for each correct answer.*

1. Who did Scully see meet The Cigarette-Smoking Man in the motel parking lot?
2. What did Patnik record for his video library?
3. What did Mrs. Helene Riddick mistake for a beautiful blond woman?
4. Which contemporary political figure did Scully end up watching on videotape?
5. To whom does Mulder entrust the analysis of the device found in the cable box?

Tougher Trivia: *These are two-pointers all the way.*

6. What did Sylvia, the game-show contestant, win?
7. What famous trial was shown while Mulder watched Patnik's video collection?
8. Name the figurine Mulder found in front of Mrs. Riddick's television?
9. How old was Joseph Patnik when he killed his wife?
10. Name the "modern-day Hitler" who made Joseph Patnik "wiggy."

According to William Gaines, a psychology professor tracking the way people respond to changing technology, "We're in the midst of rapid changes in technological ability, playing catch-up to a certain extent, determining what parts of the electronic smorgasbord will actually be useful. It's also a time when public opinion of government and politicians has hit an all-time low. The combination of those two circumstances creates an environment where subliminals are viewed with considerable suspicion."

While no one has—to public knowledge—ever attempted using subliminals on the delicate level portrayed in "Wet Wired," this particular form of persuasion continued to be used long after audiences finally saw the "Eat Popcorn" and "Drink Coke" messages placed in their films. Frohike's favorite, the "naked lady in the ice cube," probably does exist in some ad somewhere. The most famous of the ice cube tricks, however, was perpetrated in 1971 by Gilbey's gin. Hidden amid the ice cubes was the word, "sex." And despite significant public complaints, Gilbey's isn't even the latest to have done it. With the advent of digitized images, viewers can eyeball ads, television, and movies on a frame-by-frame basis, and more than one person has reported seeing "sex" written in the star patterns of that most wholesome of children's movies, *The Lion King*.

Nor are movies the only venue for subliminals.

Video-game makers included "You're A Winner" and "Play Again!" at strategic points in game play.

ANSWERS:

1. Mulder.
2. Hundreds of hours of cable news programs.
3. A dog.
4. Pat Buchanan.
5. The Lone Gunmen.
6. A washer and dryer.
7. The Menendez trial.
8. "The Little Traveler."
9. According to the paper sent by X, he was forty-six.
10. Ladoslav Miriskovic.

YOUR SCORE _____

Like the animators who slipped sly, and even X-rated, material into *Who Framed Roger Rabbit*, dozens of computer programmers continue their version of an in-joke by inserting odd or erotic images into screen-savers, background graphics, and the white spaces around words in screenfuls of text. The latest program to come under scrutiny, Windows '95, is said to include scenes of nude women amid the clouds of a bitmap used as wallpaper. If you can't find them, try looking for the couple in the new Windows logo.

The annoying Muzak commonly played in malls and department stores frequently contains voices other than those of the singers. "Don't steal" weaves its way through Nana Mouskouri's latest tune. "Treat yourself" bops along with "respect yourself." The oddest Muzak message to date, though, is likely one insinuated into the music of a notoriously slow elevator in a forty-seven-story office building in Asia: "Please don't pass wind in here."

If this seems more amusing than dangerous, the Consumer Coalition Against Subliminals in Advertising points to its own research into performers Judas Priest, Ozzy Osbourne, Alice Cooper, and other hard rockers. According to past president Colin Beech, covert messages in their music may have contributed to the suicide deaths of seven teens. The Priest and Osbourne cases were dropped for insufficient evidence, but, seven years later, there's still no clear consensus on how effective subliminals are, or whether they have any effect at all. Numerous studies have provided an amazing variety of results.

In 1987, Culligan and Harding, psychology professors, treated their students to a viewing of *Blue Lagoon*. Instead of the expected thoughts of sex, and in spite of an abundance of on-screen water, the students spent their break racing for the water fountains. After being shown the subliminal images inserted every twenty-fourth frame—of dripping faucets, glasses of water, and sand dunes—those 118 students were firmly convinced something unusual was at work.

Still, a 1989 experiment by Dr. Christian Clein, designed to play on the natural hunger of dieters, and performed under considerably more controlled circumstances, failed to elicit so much as a tummy growl or a single drop of saliva.

When Spangenbery, Obermiller, and Greenwald studied the effectiveness of subliminal self-help tapes, they discovered two interesting, and related, phenomena. First, despite the careful use of double-blind setups and placebos, the experiments failed to discover a correlation between subliminal messages and effects. When some tapes—for example, a relaxation tape and an exercise prompter—were deliberately mislabeled, the volunteer subjects frequently claimed some effect that matched the label, but no one reported an effect that corresponded to the real subliminals. What Spangenbery and company seemed to prove was that, after investing their $14.95, most people were determined to convince themselves they hadn't wasted their money.

For sheer scope and size—and, many claim, the fairest representation of the effects of subliminals—Rochester and Winston hold the record. Between 1987 and 1993, they interviewed *1,725* subjects, designed six experimental setups that passed peerage review without question, and determined that approximately 81 percent of the public respond to subliminal messages and images, 64 percent of any given audience will have a moderate reaction, and 14 percent will have swift and marked responses to such messages.

When the messages are as socially acceptable as "Don't steal," it's difficult to see any harm in them. In fact, prisons, mental hospitals, and childbirth clinics quickly came under scrutiny as venues where such understated but consistent messages might well prove beneficial.

However, just as the results of equally conscientious researchers varied, so too do individuals present a diversity of responses to subliminals. A previously well-adjusted individual, who's maybe somewhat hesitant to speak publicly, might indeed benefit from the message "You can do anything." A psychotic sociopath might mow down the diners at a local McDonald's.

Despite the mass of research already done, we just don't know how far-reaching the effects of specific subliminal messages might be. The case presented in "Wet Wired," although beyond the scope of most present-day work, did incorporate at least one element proven to affect human emotional states: color. The fad of painting prisons bubblegum pink, while absurd on the surface, worked. In prisons containing populations of equal security risk, where other living conditions could be discounted due to high degrees of similarity, color did calm violent inmates.

The complex relationship between body and mind is only now beginning to be understood; there are more unanswered questions than answers; and if subliminals are done well, the public will never know with certainty when they're being exposed to them. Few people could be induced to take untested drugs, and considering how similar to drugs subliminals are in their intent and effects, it's hardly surprising that consumers refused to be subjected to them.

When industry journals and, later, mainstream organs like *The Los Angeles Times* revealed that Director William Friedkin was admitting to using subliminals throughout the mystery thriller *Jade*, directors, production companies, and distributors found themselves answering pointed questions. Not everyone liked the answers they were giving out. People certainly weren't pleased to discover that other films, like *The Exorcist* and *Cruising*, had been subliminally cut to include images that would never have gotten past the censor boards. Two bills are currently being drafted asking that film studios be forced to warn audiences of the subliminals or that they be banned altogether.

In 1974, the Federal Communications Commission banned subliminal messages from all broadcast media. Americans spending Friday nights at home watching *The X-Files* should feel safe from electronic messages being beamed at them.

Of course, the FCC doesn't provide any similar assurance for those who spend Friday nights working at computer terminals, watching video games, or going out for a film. So if, when *The X-Files* film does come out, you find yourself thinking a second jumbo popcorn mightn't go astray, or that Coke might be a nice change from Pepsi, you may have discovered, as James Vicary claims to have done, that "Eat Popcorn" and "Drink Coca-Cola" upped sales of popcorn 57.5 percent and Coke by 18.1 percent, which may be the ultimate statement about subliminals and their effectiveness.

Always assuming, of course, that Vicary, later turned marketing consultant, later to earn some $4.5 million ($22.5 million in today's economy), and later to disappear without leaving a forwarding address, didn't play with his results, as well as with his patrons' minds. Stuart Rogers, a researcher with a bent for digging deeply into claims such as Vicary's, has made a convincing case for the notion that Vicary never conducted the famous "Popcorn Experiment."

If subliminals don't work as well as has been reported, at least one modern game maker has been taken for a ride. Time Warner advertised Endorfun, a computer game described as a cross between Tetris and brainwashing, as a game that not only entertains but "promotes positive self-images." Players are treated to a high-quality CD-ROM game, without the violence common to so many recent releases, offering forty-two different games (with 500 play levels), that subject the viewer to a variety of subliminals.

> *I am a winner.*
> *I am at peace.*
> *I can do anything.*
> *My heart is filled with joy.*

If the next generation of gamers turns out to be happier, better-adjusted players, perhaps we'll finally have the definitive answer to the question of subliminal messaging.

eXtras:

Did you catch the *Jeopardy* reference in this episode? Check out Mrs. Riddick's video collection and you'll see a prominent cassette with "Jeopardy" scrawled across the label.

Although X-Philes have been waiting since "Beyond the Sea" for another glimpse of the remaining Scully men, they were disappointed once again in "Wet Wired." Only Scully and Melissa were recognizable among the family photos on Mrs. Scully's bedside table. The brothers remain an X-File in their own right, though the identity of the child in Sheila Larken's (Mrs. Scully) arms is no mystery to her. The photo is one of her own, featuring her own child.

Tachlstoscope: (n.) device used by Vicary to flash light and images at 1/60,000th of a second intervals.

X

Vicary's Popcorn Experiment was conducted at a drive-in theater at Fort Lee, New Jersey, but a variety of sources have set it erroneously, in nearby Grover's Mill. Fans of *The X-Files* may remember that as the locale for "War of the Coprophages." Long-time science fiction buffs, of course, also recognize the reference to Orson Welles's classic radio-play about the Martian invasion fleet, "War of the Worlds."

 Blooper Alert! In the opening scenes of this episode, we see a nifty "reflection" of the Capitol Building. But with Mulder's car sitting on a street with three-story buildings on both sides, where could the source of the reflection, the Capitol Building itself, possibly be?

X

Blooper Alert! Though Mulder claimed to have watched thirty-six hours of tapes on fast forward, the last tape he removes from the machine was never actually *in* the machine. It was just laid there for appearances and the signal was piped in from an outside source.

CODE NAME: "TALITHA CUMI"

CASE SUMMARY:

After arriving at what should be a bloody crime scene, Mulder and Scully are astounded to find that the gunman's victims have been miraculously healed and that their mysterious benefactor eluded questioning by "just disappearing." The hunt for Jeremiah Smith intensifies when Scully discovers a series of identical men, hauntingly similar to the cloned Gregors, stretching across the country.

EYEWITNESS STATEMENT:

"Men can never be free because they're weak, corrupt, worthless, and restless. The People believe in authority. They've grown tired of waiting for miracle and mystery. Science is their religion. No greater explanation exists for them. They must never believe any differently if the Project is to go forward."

—The Cigarette-Smoking Man

David Duchovny and
Cigarette-Smoking Man,
William B. Davis

In the Beginning—and the End!

If there are three words that strike horror in the TV-viewing public's heart, they have to be "To Be Continued . . ."

With those few words tacked so cruelly to the end of "Anasazi," the X-Philean world had been plunged into the four-month-long wait between seasons, a near-intolerable period for the truly dedicated fan who was left wondering if, or how, Special Agent Fox Mulder could escape from a burning boxcar in a remote corner of Navajo reservation. Thinking to equal if not exceed last season's cliff-hanger ending, the X-crew provided its audience with several much more insidious questions to ponder under the summer sunshine: Was *The X-Files*, becoming infamous for paying "homage" to classic sci-fi and horror through imitation, actually going to pull a *Star Wars* ending? Was the angst-ridden Fox Mulder about to discover his nemesis was none other than his father? Was the mother he'd tucked so tenderly into bed—

TRIVIA BUSTER 25

Easy Stuff: *Take a single point for each correct answer.*

1. For what illness was Mrs. Mulder hospitalized?
2. Where did Mulder find the "switchpick"?
3. What one-word message did Mrs. Mulder write in Scully's notebook?
4. How many people are shot in the restaurant?
5. In which prison cell is Jeremiah Smith confined?

Tougher Trivia: *These are two-pointers all the way.*

6. For what agency did Jeremiah Smith work?
7. What station provided Mulder with tape of Jeremiah Smith?
8. Who, besides himself, did Jeremiah Smith appear to be during his interrogation?
9. Where did the Mulder family have a summer house?
10. What "diagnosis" does Jeremiah Smith deliver to The Cigarette-Smoking Man?

precipitating endless Oedipus discussions in X-Philean circles—also his enemy's former lover?

Speculation ran rampant, outperforming "Who killed Laura Palmer?" and "Who shot J.R.?" Taped copies began to blur as X-Philes everywhere awaited the September conclusion—and their next deep breath. In a bid to release the tension, X-Philes dug in, found another crumb of patience, and discovered a way to relieve the tension of all the two- and three-parters. In a regularly recurring, episode-after-episode, run-to-the-end season series of conspiracies, monsters, and sheer terror, desperate fans got through the off-season hiatus and commercial breaks alike with The UnOfficial X-Files Drinking Game. (For those under the legal drinking age, substitute Gummi Bears, M&M's, or, for a touch of nostalgia, sunflower seeds. In any case, don't attempt to operate vehicles or heavy machinery for several days after a marathon of *The X-Files* episodes!)

ANSWERS:

1. A stroke.
2. Inside a lamp.
3. PALM.
4. Four. Three by Galen Muntz, then Galen himself.
5. B18.
6. The Social Security Administration.
7. WZCO, Channel 11.
8. William Mulder and Deep Throat.
9. Quonochontuag, Rhode Island. (Give yourself an extra point if you spelled it correctly!)
10. Smith claims The Cigarette-Smoking Man has lung cancer.

YOUR SCORE _____

The Unofficial X-Files Drinking Game

STEP ONE: Set the stage.

- Collect as many episodes as you think you can view comfortably in a single evening.
- Arrange your beverage or snack of choice in a convenient location. Elbow-bending distance is recommended.
- Turn out the lights.
- Make sure *you've* got control of the remote.

STEP TWO: Listen closely. This is where the fun starts!

Take a single sip, or snack, when any of the following happens:

- Anyone says, "I don't know!"
- Scully rolls her eyes.
- Mulder provides a theory that stuns his partner.
- A language other than English, or subtitles, is used.
- Scully or Mulder says, "It's me."
- Mulder is called anything other than "Mulder."
- The Cigarette-Smoking Man squints out through a haze of smoke from his own cigarette.
- Mulder loses his gun or cellular phone.
- Our favorite agents use their super-duper flashlights.
- Any character sees/eats/mentions sunflower seeds.
- Scully performs a postmortem exam on a human cadaver.
- Mulder, Scully, or any of their colleagues messes up the science.
- A character known only by a descriptive name (i.e., The Cigarette-Smoking Man) turns up during an investigation.
- There's a close-up of Scully's feet.
- An alternative-music tune plays in the background.
- Mulder and/or Scully runs afoul of local law enforcement officers.
- Scully or Mulder sticks something into a specimen bottle.
- You find yourself reaching for the dictionary after watching *The X-Files*.
- Any character investigates anything alone.

If you hear/see any of these, take two sips or two treats:

- Scully explains the bleeding obvious.
- A string of numbers that looks like it ought to mean *something*.
- Uniformed men, carrying guns and ready to chase down our heroes, appear at the order of a mysterious man.
- Scully and/or Mulder rents a car from Lariat Rent-A-Car.
- Mulder alludes to his pornography collection or interest.
- Someone sticks a masking-tape X in a window.
- "Abduction" and "Samantha" are mentioned in the same speech by any regularly appearing character.
- Scully performs a postmortem examination on anything *other* than an obviously human cadaver.
- A helicopter makes its appearance.
- Anyone is attacked in a bathroom.
- Scully and Mulder get DNA/PCR testing results back in less than twenty-four hours.
- One character calls another an SOB.
- A dead character appears under "unusual" circumstances.
- Any "aliens" appear.
- We're treated to pictures of something seen through a microscope.
- Mrs. Mulder sniffles.
- Scully or Mulder wears glasses.
- Camera pulls a close-up on a clock.
- Anyone alludes to the "Roswell incident."
- Mulder appears to forget he has a psychology degree, or Scully forgets her own undergraduate degree in physics.
- Someone quotes from the Bible.

These rare occurrences rate a big gulp or a handful of junk food:

- Scully agrees with Mulder.
- Mulder addresses Scully as anything other than "Scully."
- Scully and Mulder find themselves in a dark room with anything *other* than their super-duper flashlights.
- The credits include a phrase other than "THE TRUTH IS OUT THERE."
- Mulder or Scully encounters a former lover.

- Any of the regulars appear without all their street clothes.
- One of the Mulders or Scullys is murdered.
- Any character is hypnotized.
- Something blows up.
- Someone under investigation turns out to have a bipolar condition.
- Mulder and Scully receive unconditional support for their investigations from local law enforcement personnel.
- Dead animals make an appearance.

If any of these happen to come up, turn off the tape (or TV), find a friend, and go out for a real evening, because it's all over anyway!

- The one-and-only, uncloned, Samantha Mulder is found.
- Mulder presents Congress with irrefutable proof of the existence of Extraterrestrial Biological Entities.
- Scully and Mulder end up in bed together.

STEP THREE: Invite in the next group of victims and see Step One.

STEP FOUR: Keep this list handy for the next season-ending cliffhanger, the long stretch of reruns, or the inevitable Sweeps Week two-parters.

eXtras:

Catch the name of the restaurant? "Brothers K" is a reference to *The Brothers Karamazov*, a novel by Fyodor Dostoyevsky. The scenes between The Cigarette-Smoking Man and the incarcerated Jeremiah Smith are inspired by the chapter "The Grand Inquisitor."

Find the notion of The Cigarette-Smoking Man on water skis amusing? Well, William B. Davis, the actor who portrays The Cigarette-Smoking Man, was the Canadian National Water Ski Champion in his younger days.

Talitha cumi. From the Aramaic: "Arise, Maiden!"

X-REFERENCE:

Getting to Know You

Over the course of three seasons and seventy-plus episodes, audiences expect characters to develop their little oddities of action, personal idiosyncracies, likes, dislikes, and other emotional baggage. However, when an attractive young agent seems bent on cutting up every cadaver she runs across, despite the plethora of perfectly good state and county coroners already employed for just that purpose, audiences would have to be forgiven for wondering how she spends her off hours.

Scully really needs a new hobby.

Season One

X **Pilot:**
On their first case together, Scully, who'd apparently never been involved in the exhumation of a body before, begins what will be a long and personal association with corpses by performing the autopsy on the body of "Ray Soames," or a chimpanzee . . . or an orangutan . . . or . . .

X **"Shadows":**
As if she won't rack up enough hours in the morgue, even the CIA has her looking over bodies! In this case, the corpses of two would-be muggers who had the misfortune to try robbing Lauren Kyte. However, the notable feature of these deaths—that the throats were crushed from the inside—had already been determined.

X **"Ice":**
"Ice" provided Scully with more autopsy practice than any other case as she examined the bodies of all six of those originally killed at the Arctic Ice Core Project installation as well as those of Bear and Denny. Eight bodies found their way into body bags and cold storage before they left, and only some interesting research techniques prevented the project's pooch from joining the list.

X **"Miracle Man":**
Despite the objections of an evangelical church, Scully finally manages to autopsy one of the many supplicants to die under the eyes of the Miracle Ministry. As she suspected, the victim, Margaret Homan, didn't die from the "laying on of hands." Poison, more direct and reliable, was what Scully determined was the official cause of death.

X **"Born Again":**
Detective Barbala was the next to fall under Scully's knife after his dive out of a police-station window while in the company of Michelle Bishop. It may have seemed like a waste of time to Scully—after all, the only evidence of any value, an electrocution-style lesion, had already been predicted by her partner.

Season Two

X **"Little Green Men":**
Even when Mulder isn't dragging her into newer, more bizarre cases, Scully can't seem to get rid of those hideous medical greens. Reassigned to Quantico after the X-Files are closed, Scully learns that her first on-screen task is to conduct an autopsy for the benefit of the next generation of agents.

X **"The Host":**
You'd almost think that Scully would have had enough of the autopsy bay by the time the second season rolled around. After all, she'd been averaging a body a month for the previous year and was already playing show-and-tell with another batch of cadavers for the benefit of her students. Apparently not. In "The Host," she *asks* to autopsy one of the grossest corpses to date, the one harboring a miniature Flukeman.

X **"Blood":**
It seems Mulder took Scully's volunteering to autopsy his Corpse-To-Go as a sign of enthusiasm, something to be continued even after Scully escaped the confines of Quantico's demonstration labs. Mrs. MacRoberts, the housewife who'd seemed intent on attempting a *pre-mortem* exam on Mulder before she herself was shot, is the first of a long string of bodies to cross Scully's table in upcoming episodes.

X **"Sleepless":**
Continuing his practice of treating bodies as something that could be "wrapped to go," Mulder literally sends Scully one of her oddest cases yet. Dr. Grissom, despite all the physical evidence to the contrary, exhibits all the biological evidence required to engage Scully's curiosity. Of course, how much curiosity would it really take to distract her from the second of her How-To-Chop-'Em-Up classes?

X **"Firewalker":**
Even her abduction, a life-shaking incident if ever there was one, didn't break the old habit of mucking about inside dead bodies. Despite a rather marked lack of facilities, Scully manages an incredibly

extensive postmortem on Tanaka, identifying a previously unknown organism with nothing more than a geology lab at her disposal. Not a bad effort for a woman on her first case in months and only recently returned from the dead herself. Still, she was probably delighted when Trepkos thoroughly incinerated Ludwig down in the steam caves. *The X-Files'* crew does have a taste for the bizarre, and that coated-condom prosthetic must have made working with a straight face difficult enough.

X "Irresistible":

"Irresistible" was something of a revelation to most Scully fans. Having spent nearly two years making the "autopsy scene" a by-the-numbers routine, the writers threw the audience a curve. Mulder may wax poetic under a field of stars, but Scully's rare moment of introspection, when she *finally* shows *some* reaction to the dramatic and intrusive events since meeting Duane Barry, occurs over the disfigured body of a hooker.

X "Fresh Bones":

Despite her emotional reaction to the bodies she encountered in "Irresistible," Scully once again appears perfectly comfortable while demanding to personally view the body of a young soldier whose cause of death was a mundane car crash. Of course, finding a dead dog where her cadaver is supposed to be sort of changes her mind on any immediate postmortem exams. That was probably a lucky thing in the long run, what with the cadaver actually being alive and all.

X "Colony":

Perhaps having your autopsy subjects walk out on you makes you a little less anxious to be the one doing the original exam. In "Colony," despite Mulder's suggestion that she procure an autopsy bay for the examination of a deceased agent, Scully seems content just to observe the corpse and depend on the official results of a previous autopsy.

X "Fearful Symmetry":

Despite the fact that Scully won't darken the doorway of an autopsy theater for several weeks, she doesn't completely escape the rigors of searching for evidence on the insides of her victims. In a makeshift morgue, Scully finds herself literally neck-deep in her next and largest subject by removing an elephant's uterine tissue for examination. In a career filled with autopsies, this one necropsy will likely stand as the weirdest, the messiest, and the most productive of her forays into the dead. This time, Scully finally finds a cut-and-dried answer: Yes, the elephant was pregnant. Still, as she showers off afterward, she must wonder if that answer is worth the experience of standing inside the three-day-old body of a decomposing elephant.

X   **"Humbug":**
Curiosity, however, gets the better of her yet again in "Humbug," proving once and for all that the circus *is* the ultimate in entertainment, with something for everyone—even someone who spends her off-camera moments deep in other people's entrails. After all, how often does a girl get to observe, up close, the insides of a man who acts as a motel to a dislocating twin?

X   **"Our Town":**
It's almost back to business as usual in "Our Town" when Scully, through a routine autopsy of Paula Gray, discovers a perfectly down-to-earth, untailored, nondesigner, and traditionally diagnosable, if rare, disease at work.

> "Well, I think an autopsy on Paula Gray would clarify things."
>
> —Scully

X   **"D.P.O.":**
Darren Oswald's unusual method of killing his victims leaves some interesting evidence for Scully to examine, and examine it she does—despite the fact that the work was already completed once by the assigned county coroner, and despite the fact that her only reason for spending the morning looking at fried cataracts and well-done heart muscles is her partner's request that she do so. Maybe she is just grateful that Mulder doesn't expect her to do repeat examinations on the dead cows, too.

"Clyde Bruckman's Final Repose":

It probably doesn't require a psychic to guess that, with a body available, Scully will once again spend her morning in oversized disposable clothes and latex gloves—but it's a nice touch in "CBFR."

Though someone else appears to have conducted the majority of the autopsies on the murdered prognosticators, Scully just can't resist getting in on the action and tags along for the autopsy of a tea-leaf-reading doll collector dragged out of a lake next to a "Nazi storm trooper."

"The List":

Considering the number of bodies arising from "The List," Scully shows admirable restraint throughout this case, restricting herself to suggesting the official pathologist get bodies into the fridge before the maggots destroy whatever evidence may be available. Even when they eventually find the body to match the decapitated head already sitting in the prison morgue, Scully ignores Mulder's gibes and lets someone else handle the growing stack of bodies. In a rather amazing departure, Scully doesn't autopsy any one of the five men from Neech's list.

"2SHY":

Again, it's almost back to the same routine when Scully decides to conduct the autopsy on Lauren MacKalvey and, in the process, displaces the area's usual pathologist, Dr. Kramer, and upsets the delicate sensibilities of fellow investigator Detective Cross. The point is almost made moot by the gradual dissolution of the victim's body—which may explain Dr. Kramer's odd willingness to hand over the lab to an outsider.

"Revelations":

Scully's morgue comfort level drops abruptly in "Revelations" when the religious beliefs of her youth seem to be coming true on the autopsy table. "St. Owen," as Mulder dubs the unusual man who only wanted to "go to Heaven," haunts Scully in ways the most grotesque corpses don't. Religion in the closed confines of the confessional is, apparently, one thing, but religion rearing its head in the sterile, scientific arena of the morgue is another matter altogether. Morgues just aren't supposed to smell of fresh roses.

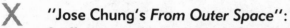

"Jose Chung's *From Outer Space*":
Scully's own close encounter in an Ohio morgue with an apparently incorruptible corpse appears to have dampened her enthusiasm for such pursuits; at least she doesn't step into the autopsy bay again until "Jose Chung's *From Outer Space*," in which her subject is anything *but* supernatural. Discovering zippers and rubber heads while becoming the leading live star of "Dead Alien!: Truth or Humbug" just isn't a good career move. She stays out of the autopsy bay for the rest of this one.

"Avatar":
Scully's next trip into the disinfected atmosphere of the autopsy theater is less than satisfying. Feeling personally compelled by the alleged involvment of Assistant Director Walter Skinner in the murder of a hotel pickup girl, she diligently reviews the findings of previous pathologists, attempts to retrieve that episode's "weird and unanalyzable" substance, and drags her partner back to skeptically eye a now-normal-looking cadaver, all for nothing. Despite applying every resource of the department and all her own open-mindedness, her efforts do nothing more than give her superiors cause to claim she's tampered with evidence in an attempt to inject that "shadow of a doubt" on Skinner's guilt. It seems politics, as well as religion, can be discovered amid the organs and preservatives.

Seventy-two cases later, Scully has opened and closed no less than twenty men, seven women, one elephant, and one unknown which may or may not have been an orangutan. Not bad for a field agent with absolutely no authority within the Coroner's Office, no standing with any hospital, and no laboratory responsibility within the Bureau.

Trivia Buster Scorecard

So? Think you're ready to send in that application to the FBI, huh? Think you'll be allowed to pursue your own pet projects? Add up those scores first—no cheating!—and see where you fit into the Grand Scheme of Things.

1–25	Hmmm, how to put this politely . . . ? The Lone Gunman on a skating rink would be less conspicuous than you! Get yourself back to Basic Training; beg, borrow or steal the carefully hoarded collection of video tape lurking around the VCRs of true X-Philes—and take notes this time!
26–100	Thanks, but we can't help but feel you'd be better suited to some other branch of the Service—preferably with someone else's government! Is the Foreign Legion still taking applicants?
101–150	Well, if they hadn't upped the entrance requirements to 70 percent, you just might have made it. Perhaps a tutor could get you through, at least help you survive dinner table conversations on the most popular show of the '90s.
151–200	You're not likely to be the "golden-haired boy" at Quantico, but still, you might well "distinguish" yourself there and, after all, the Agent Pendrells and Agent Danny Bernsteins are the real heart of the agency, right?
201–225	Yes! With your keen powers of observation, your incredible memory, your ability to link disparate bits of information, you are the future of the Bureau! Ah, just one thing: you didn't happen to misplace a sister when you were twelve, did you?
226–?	Excuse me, but could you step in here? Ignore that security clearance notice. You see, we keep an eye out for people with your . . . talents. Who are we? We don't have names . . .

About the Author

N. E. Genge is the author of *The Unofficial X-Files Companion I* and a principal source of *X-Files* lore and insider information on the World Wide Web. Her short fiction has been published in *Asimov* and *Story* magazines. She lives in Newfoundland, Canada.